TAKING BETTE

VIDEOS

GW00382130

Achieving professional style and impact

CASSELL

ACKNOWLEDGEMENTS
Front cover; (main) Zefa, (left inset, centre inset, right inset) Kos Photos, 1 ICL/Horizon, 2-3 Sylvia Cordaiy Picture Library/Nick Rains, 4,5 ICL, 6 ICL/Horizon, 7(l) Rosalinda McGovern/Eaglemoss, 7(r) Sue Jenkins/Peter Coomb, 8 Steve Tanner/Eaglemoss, 9 Colin Garrett, 10 Paul Minoli/Eaglemoss, 11 TPL, 12 Zefa, 13 Kos Photos, 14 Paul Minoli/Eaglemoss, 15 TIB, 16, 17(l) Shona Wood/Eaglemoss, 17(r) TSI, 18 Shona Wood/Eaglemoss, 19 TIB, 20(t) Allsport/J.Daniel, 20(b) Shona Wood/Eaglemoss, 21(t) TIB, 21(c,bl) Zefa, 22 Shona Wood/Eaglemoss, 23-30 Shona Wood/Eaglemoss, 31(t) Steve Tanner/Eaglemoss, 31(c,b), 32 Shona Wood/Eaglemoss, 34 Steve Tanner/Eaglemoss, 35, 36(b) Simon Page-Ritchie/Eaglemoss, 36(t) Shona Wood/Eaglemoss, 37 Shona Wood, 38 Steve Parker, 39 Shona Wood/Eaglemoss, 40(t) Chris Lees, 40(b), 41-46 Shona Wood/Eaglemoss, 47 Allsport/Adrian Murrell, 48(b) TPL, 48(t), 49, 50 Shona Wood/Eaglemoss, 51(t) TSI, 51(b) RHPL, 52-53 Steve Tanner/Eaglemoss, 54 John Suett/Eaglemoss, 55(t) TIB, 55(cr) Trevor Melton/Eaglemoss, 55(bl) Roger Howard, 55(br) TIB, 56(t) TSI, 56(b), 57(t,b) Shona Wood/Eaglemoss, 57(c) Steve Tanner/Eaglemoss, 58 Tim Woodcock, 59(t) TIB, 59(c) Shona Wood/Eaglemoss, 59(b) George Wright, 60, 61(r) Shona Wood/Eaglemoss, 61(l), 62, 63 Trevor Melton/Eaglemoss, 64 Shona Wood/Eaglemoss, 65(tr) Simon Page-Ritchie/Eaglemoss, 65(b) TSI, 66(t) TIB, 66(b) RHPL, 67 Trevor Melton/Eaglemoss, 68 Simon Page-Ritchie/Eaglemoss, 69-71, 73(insets) Shona Wood/Eaglemoss, 73, 74 Simon Page-Ritchie/Eaglemoss, 75, 76(t) Shona Wood/Eaglemoss, 76(b) Simon Page-Ritchie/Eaglemoss, 77-83, 84(t) Shona Wood/Eaglemoss, 84(b) Trevor Melton/Eaglemoss, 85-88 Shona Wood/Eaglemoss, 89 Bruce Coleman/Hans Reinhard, 90 Ardea, 91(t) Bruce Coleman/Eric Crichton, 91(b) Ardea/Francois Gohier, 92(t) Sylvia Cordaiy/Nigel Rolstone, 92(c) Bruce Coleman/George McCarthy, 92(bl) Bruce Coleman/Hans Reinhard, 92(br) Shona Wood/Eaglemoss, 93(t) Zefa, 93(c) Reflections/Jennifer Woodcock, 93(b) Sally and Richard Greenhill, 94 Trevor Melton/Eaglemoss, 95(t) Hanimex-Vivitar, 95(bl) Johnsons Photopia, 95(br) Kodak, 96(t) Zefa, Back cover Shona Wood/Eaglemoss.

Key: RHPL - Robert Harding Picture Library; TIB - The Image Bank;
TPL - The Photographers Library; TSI - Tony Stone Images

Consultant editor: Roger Hicks

First published 1993 by Cassell
Villiers House, 41/47 Strand, London WC2N 5JE

Copyright © Cassell 1993
Based on *Camera Wise*
Copyright © Eaglemoss Publications Ltd 1993

All rights reserved. No part of this book may be reproduced or transmitted in any form or by any means, electronic or mechanical, including photocopying, recording or any information storage and retrieval system, without prior permission in writing from the copyright holder and Publisher.

Distributed in Australia
by Capricorn Link (Australia) Pty Ltd
P. O. Box 665, Lane Cove, NSW 2066

British Library Cataloguing-in-Publication Data
A catalogue record for this book is available from the British Library

ISBN 0-304-34353-6

Printed in Spain by Cayfosa Industria Grafica

CONTENTS

INTRODUCTION

LET'S be honest: we rarely want to watch other people's home videos. And yet, you think nothing of flicking on the television and watching what are, after all, professional versions of the same thing. What is the difference?

The vast majority of home videos are hard to follow and go on for too long. Some of them make you seasick as well, as the viewpoint waves and weaves all over the place like a hosepipe and the lens zooms in and out like a trombone. Making successful home videos is not simply a question of buying a high-quality camcorder and pointing it at your subject. You have to have a reason for pointing it where you do; you have to have something to tell the people who are going to see the video; and you have to know how to hold their interest.

Because camcorders are so very easy to use, many people never bother to learn more than how to operate the controls; which is a bit like a toddler hammering the keys of a typewriter with tiny fists and saying "I can type! I can type!" Like the typewriter, the camcorder is basically a tool for communicating, and you can use that tool well or badly.

In fact, learning to make good videos is rather like learning to write good English. We talk of the "universal language" of moving pictures and, like any language, video has its grammar. Individual shots are like sentences, and sequences of shots are like paragraphs. The whole video is like a magazine article, or a short story. We "edit" video just as we "edit" the written word, pruning out the errors and irrelevant material so that we tell a story with a beginning, a middle, and an end. A well-written story, or a well-written letter for that matter, does not ramble on without saying anything, and then suddenly stop; and nor does a well-made video.

The story or theme is really the heart of the matter. Any good film or TV programme begins with a "hook" which captures your attention; goes on to give you more information which builds on your initial interest; and finally ends with some sort of conclusion, which sums the whole thing up in a satisfying way. All the way through, the pictures and the soundtrack are both clear and comprehensible, and nothing stays on the screen long enough to bore you.

No book would guarantee to make you into a second Shakespeare or Balzac, and we cannot promise that we can turn you into an award-winning video maker. But we can assure you that, if you master the straightforward techniques explained in this book, you will learn to fully utilize your creative potential to achieve a much more professional effect.

Whether you want to document your everyday life, make a record of your family growing up, or create an intensely personal vision of the world, you will find that these pages contain all the information you need to make videos which other people actually want to watch.

Welcome to video

Most people get into video by hiring or borrowing a camcorder for a weekend and playing around with it. With some basic principles to guide you, you'll be surprised what good results you achieve straight away – and how quickly you can improve on them.

The bonus of taking up video is that you're already something of an expert – you've watched countless films and television programmes. Years of exposure to cinema and TV give you a good grounding in video technique without you ever being aware of it.

Next time you're watching TV, notice how you automatically know when a few hours or even days have passed between scenes. You are aware of who is going to perform the next action and you can sense when something is going to happen. You are not telepathic but simply responding to familiar and well understood film-making signals.

Watch the ads on television

You can learn a lot by watching TV commercials. Most last only 30-60 seconds, but notice how many different shots they contain. In that short time, they have to hold your attention and get across a clear message – try to do the same in your videos.

Professional cameramen follow a set of quite straightforward rules and a knowledge of these can turn passive awareness of what you are viewing into active mastery of moving image techniques.

Experience of stills photography also helps. You are already used to looking at the world through a viewfinder, choosing a good camera angle and thinking about light and shadow. But video calls for extra skills.

A photograph is complete in itself: a video incorporates movement, time, speed and sound. It is a collection of sequences, each containing a number of shots. Each shot needs to be connected to what went before and what is coming next.

◀▲ The wedding videomaker plays a key role – everyone looks forward to viewing the big day on screen. But technical knowhow, practice and planning make all the difference between a piece of fun and a permanent treasure.

Tape format and camera size

There are six formats – six types of cassette which have to be compatible with the camcorder used. The three basic formats are VHS, VHS-C and 8mm.
Each of these has a 'hi-band' companion, using the same cassette size but better quality tape and camcorder electronics to improve picture quality. Hi-band machines, which are more expensive, should be plugged into TV sets with special S-connectors (S for Super) to maximize picture quality.

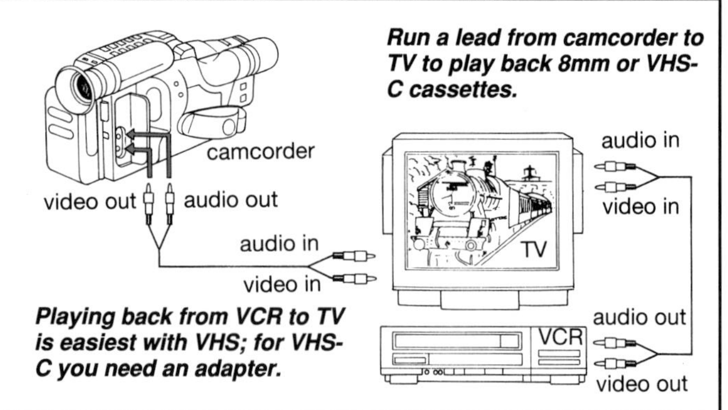

Run a lead from camcorder to TV to play back 8mm or VHS-C cassettes.

Playing back from VCR to TV is easiest with VHS; for VHS-C you need an adapter.

Camcorder size

Large size – VHS shoulder mounted

Average weight range: 2.3-3.5kg

These machines are the easiest to hold steady, but tiring to use over long periods and heavy to carry about. Expensive to buy new, you can get cheap secondhand models.

▶ ***The right hand holds the hand grip and operates the record and power zoom buttons. The left hand steadies the camcorder and operates less frequently used controls such as backlight. It also focuses or zooms the lens when you are operating it manually.***

How to hold

Compatible formats

VHS cassettes
VHS camcorders use standard VHS cassettes – the same size you use in a video recorder. These cassettes are the cheapest and give a long playing time – 3 to 4 hours. Hi-band equivalent: S-VHS.

Medium size – VHS-C and 8mm hand held

Average weight range: 1-1.5kg

Though light enough to be operated with one hand, it's not advisable as you may shake the machine. These camcorders are cheaper than large design models.

▶ ***These neat and versatile machines are best held between both hands.***

VHS-C format
VHS-C tape is the same as that used in VHS cassettes. But the cassettes are smaller and the playing time shorter – up to 45 minutes at Standard Speed (SP) or 1½ hours in long play (LP). You need an adapter to play back on most video recorders, or you can run a lead from the camcorder to the TV. Hi-band equivalent: S-VHS-C.

Small size – VHS-C and 8mm palmcorder

Average weight range: 790g-1kg

Palmcorders are so tiny they can be packed in a small briefcase or even a handbag. But their small size makes them more prone to shake, so always support them with both hands when recording.

▶ ***These are small enough to be held in one hand to scan the scene, but switch to two before you start recording.***

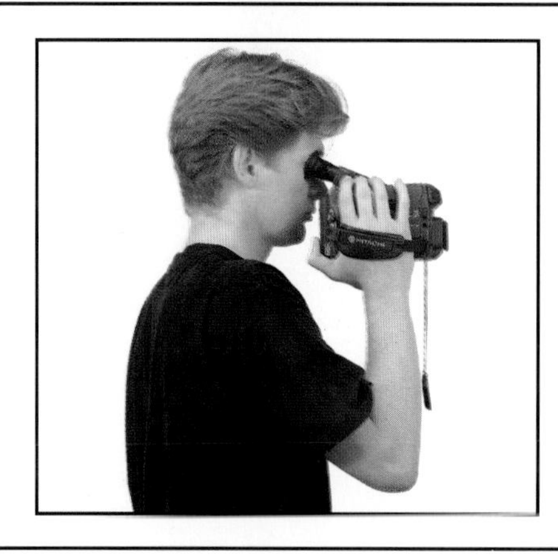

8mm cassettes
These are thinner than VHS-C cassettes, as they use narrower tape. Playing time is up to 1½ hours (SP), 3 hours (LP). Hi-band equivalent: Hi8.
There aren't many 8mm recorders around for playing back cassettes, but your camcorder can be used for this, as for VHS-C above.

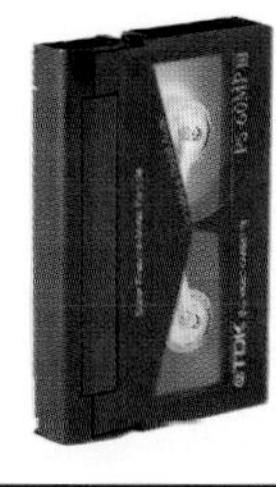

Try before you buy

Buying a camcorder is quite an investment. Prices vary not only from shop to shop, but from month to month, so have a good look around before making your choice.

If possible try out three camcorders, one of each basic size – large, medium and small. This gives you the chance to see which you are most comfortable with.

The type of camcorder you choose also depends on how much you want to spend and what you intend to use it for. Don't buy anything before thinking through what your long term plans are. If you expect to do a lot of travelling, for example, the weight and portability of your chosen camcorder may be the deciding factor.

All camcorders are fully automatic, with both autofocus and autoexposure built in: the camera takes care of everything except choosing the subject.

With camcorders you pay extra for manual overrides such as manual exposure control. If you're used to handling manual overrides with an SLR you might want to try one that gives you greater control.

Sound quality and other features are explored on pages 31-38.

Telling a story

A good video tells a story, whether it is a five minute celebration of some family fun or a full length record of a special day such as a wedding. How well the story comes across to the viewer depends on the camerawork, lighting, editing and sound recording – all factors that you can learn to manipulate.

Getting the timing right is crucial – lingering too long on a shot is the most common fault in amateur video. Watching a small girl eating ice cream – and then getting it in her hair – can hold your attention for several minutes in real life. But on a TV screen it gets boring after more than 15 seconds.

Plan your shoot first and you're less likely to end up with lots of overlong and irrelevant footage.

Planning a sequence

Scene 1

When videoing a steam train, capture the power and speed of the locomotive as it rushes by.

Scene 1 shows the engine coming into the station. Keep your angle consistent to emphasize the movement of the train against a stationary background. Start videoing a few seconds before the train comes into shot to establish the location (the signal box serves to do this). This way your viewers know what to expect – especially if the sound of the train is picked up before it comes into view.

Scene 2 makes use of a bridge to capture an interesting angle of the train.

Scene 2

Scene 3

Scene 3 – get as close as you can to the train as it rushes by. The blurring as it shoots by the camcorder emphasizes how fast it is going.

CHECK IT!

Before you start the tape turning

❑ Do you have a clear idea of what sequences you want to shoot and in what order?
❑ Have you 'briefed' your volunteers so they know what you want them to do?
❑ Have you asked them to wear bright colours that will show up well against the background?

PROJECT Washing the car

When you're trying out a camcorder for the first time, it's best to start by shooting something simple. A perfect project would be filming a couple of friends washing the car. You get plenty of action, but it all occurs in a fixed area. A bonfire scene, building a snowman or feeding ducks in the park would also do the trick.

Aim to tell a coherent story and restrict your video to about a minute. You might have to have a few goes and try 90 seconds to start with. Some shots should be only 2 or 3 seconds long.

Plan it out in 'scenes' first. Allow for something unexpected to happen – it always does! It might be a cat running across your field of vision or a neighbour coming out to chat.

Turn on the car radio, to give you some sound and help you assess the merits of the camcorder's microphone.

If you're trying out several different kinds of camcorder, shoot the same sequences on each.

Start with an opening shot that sets the scene. This shows the people ready to begin work and includes a foreground shot of the car – plan your scenes in advance to split the time evenly between washing and rinsing.

Look out for interesting moments, such as emptying the bucket of water over the car to rinse off the soap. You can shoot this whole movement, holding the shot for longer than you would when little is happening.

Make the most of any unplanned events, such as a dog entering the scene. A shot of the finished job rounds the video off nicely.

The three basic shots

How far you are from the action – and the size the subject occupies in the frame – completely alters the impact of your video. Three classic shots are the basis of every video, and a knowledge of how, why and when to use them will add real spice to your video-making skills.

All videos consist of long shots, mid shots and close-ups.

The long shot includes the whole action, the mid shot concentrates on the most important aspect of it and the close-up picks out detail.

Which shot when

There are two ways of changing from one type of shot to another. One is to pause the camcorder and move closer to or further away from the subject. The other is to use the zoom lens.

Long shots give a lot of information about a location. They are useful for opening a sequence, when they are called 'establishing shots'. They also show your subject in its environment.

Whenever you need a wide view to see all the action or to show a new location, switch to long shots. Although they're informative, use them only when necessary, as they distance the viewer from the action.

Most action takes place in the **mid shot,** so you are close enough to your subjects – usually people – to show them clearly. You can make out the expressions on their faces, but you can also see their gestures.

Mid shots leave enough room around the subject to see some of the action that surrounds them. They are often used for shots of two people so that speech and reaction can be viewed at the same time.

Close-ups focus the attention on one subject only. They are high impact shots that bring the audience a lot closer to the action emotionally and physically.

These shots are often used for strong facial reactions, or for important dialogue. The more of the face you show, the more impact it has – for instance, a shot of a pair of eyes filling the screen shocks the viewer.

Close-ups can also show the viewer details such as winking, unseen by those taking part in the scene.

▼ **LONG SHOT**
When you're videoing a person, the long shot includes the whole body. The amount of background you leave around a figure is up to you. Here, the wide space around the girl emphasizes the open location, but the shot would be classed as long even if there was far less space above the girl's head.

◀ **MID SHOT**
Here, you can see some background in the shot, but the main focus is the girl. Mid shots pick out the subject from the rest of the scene and are the most frequently used. With a figure, the mid shot is from just above the head to just below the waist – avoiding the neck, waist and knees as cut-off points.

▶ **CLOSE-UP**
Close-ups are head and shoulders shots or even closer. Home in on the face when the subject is saying something significant, or to portray emotion. The closeness of the subject makes emotion a lot stronger in close-up than in mid or long shot.

Move it!

The advantage of moving to reframe each shot is that you can get into exactly the right position every time.

The same amount of thought you put into composing a stills photograph should go into every video shot. Most shots are static – you stand still and point the camera in one direction, without zooming.

Pause the camcorder between each bit of recording and move to the best position for the next shot. This might involve you changing your viewpoint as well as your distance from the subject.

If you compose the shot while in pause mode and then switch to record, it gives the camcorder time to set the correct exposure and point of focus.

Once you've mastered this type of shot, you can move on to more advanced shots where the camera moves.

▶ ***Use the long shot to establish the scene. In this case, the lawn and kennel show that the action takes place in a garden. The kennel is more than a prop – it helps establish the importance of the dog in the video. The viewer will take in this scene and very quickly shift his eyes to the action. It might be 4-5 seconds before the viewer can absorb the whole scene. Experience helps you judge how long this usually takes.***

▼ ***As soon as the viewer's attention is resting on the main subject matter – the two children washing the dog – the video should isolate it from its surroundings. The kennel and the rest of the garden are no longer relevant. This means moving to a mid shot to concentrate on the action and get a more interesting viewpoint.***

▼ ***A close-up picks out some of the detail – the child enjoying herself and the dog having a rather less happy time of it. To show this kind of emotion, facial shots are essential. You can keep recomposing and changing your position for as long as you feel the sequence will hold the attention of anybody watching it.***

Zoom it!

All camcorders now have zoom lenses built in – most with far more power than stills cameras. This makes them very versatile tools for composition.

You can use the zoom lens either to zoom while you are in record mode or to reframe the shot while you're in pause mode. If you're reframing and you have a manual zoom control, use this to save on battery power.

A zoom is useful when you can't reframe the shot in any other way. There are many occasions when you can't get any nearer to your subject, but you want to close in on a detail.

Use the zoom sparingly. It should be chosen only when the action justifies it and not just because it's there. If you overuse it, it becomes irritating.

Opening and closing shots are prime candidates for zooms, as are any shots where action develops in one part of the frame while you're viewing it in mid or long shot.

Zooming while recording

If you want to zoom while recording, you normally zoom in from a long shot at the start of a scene and zoom out from a close-up at the end.

It is easier to start close and zoom out than it is to zoom in. If you zoom in you must make sure that your subject is properly framed in the centre of the picture when you reach the end of the zoom. You may need to practise this before recording the shot – jerky reframing towards the end of the zoom looks messy.

If the subject is moving quickly, you will have to move the camcorder with it. This is known as panning and is covered on pages 24-26.

▶ ***This is a classic situation for using a zoom. The action on the boat is interesting, as is the long shot of the vessel. Yet from the dockside you cannot vary your position and get closer to the action. By starting on the close-up you don't need to change your position during the sequence as much as if you were zooming in.***

▲ ***You have already been in the thick of the excitement aboard the boat – with the zoom you are starting to pull away from the action. By the time you get half the boat in the frame, the pace is slackening.***

▶ ***This long shot could be followed by a shot of the boat sailing away. A zoom out such as this would almost certainly be the end of a section of your video. The feeling conveyed by the zoom is that we have now left the action on the boat behind and are ready to move on to something new. The subject begins to lose its impact as its size is reduced in the frame.***

Tip: Sound sense

The lens can zoom, but the microphone can't. You can use the long telephoto to pull in very distant subjects, but the microphone picks up very few sounds that are more than two or three metres away, unless they are very noisy.

If you intend to talk over the tape or add music later this won't be a problem. Otherwise, be aware of what sounds are going on around you and whether they fit in with your subject matter.

Getting the timing right

If you have a two speed electronic zoom, use the faster speed to zoom in and the slower one to zoom out. If you zoom manually, allow more time for zooming out than zooming in. When zooming out you are revealing more of the scene to the viewer, but when you zoom in you are only closing in on something the viewer can already see.

In most situations your camcorder's automatic focusing system can cope happily with a zoom shot. There are some occasions, however, when the camcorder will have problems.

In low light give the autofocus system time to find the right subject. When you can, have a dry run before you start to record. If there is a problem, zoom more slowly. The best thing to do in these circumstances is to switch to manual focus – most camcorders allow you to do this – and set the focus yourself.

If you go from a long shot featuring a lot of bright sky to a close-up of something in shadow, this is quite a jump in light level. Using the slow electronic zoom means the camcorder's exposure system has time to adjust to the right level while you're recording.

CHECK IT!

Before you start the tape running:

- ❏ Have you worked out a good establishing shot?
- ❏ Have you thought about where to stand for a variety of viewpoints?
- ❏ Are you going to use a zoom? If so, will it be going in or out?
- ❏ Have you planned any interesting close-ups: facial expressions, washing the number plate?
- ❏ Have you thought of a good closing shot?

PROJECT Washing your car 2

You may have already made a short video of something simple, such as people washing a car. Now try it using what you've learnt about long shots, mid shots and close-ups.

Use long shots to set the scene and establish the action, mid shots to show people performing the action, and close-ups to show detail.

A zoom can be used to open or close the action, but make sure you hold the camcorder steady when you zoom, as small shakes translate to large flickers when viewed on a TV screen.

By starting and ending your short video with long shots, you give the comfortable impression of moving in to the action as it starts and moving away from it as it ends.

▲ As this video is about washing the car, it's not necessary to include all the preparation. A single long shot of the two 'stars' carrying a bucket establishes the action.

▶ Another long shot shows the car as they begin to wash it. This could be an appropriate point for a zoom to get you from the establishing shot to a close-up of the hand cleaning.

▲ A series of three quick shots – close-up, mid shot and long shot – round your video off nicely.

Framing your subject

You should compose every shot before you press the record button. This means studying the whole scene and not just the main subject.

Good composition is as important in video as in photography. However, with video, a shot lasts longer, so there is more risk of your subject moving mid shot, or some unwanted element lumbering into view.

If you are following action over which you have no control, it is impossible to ensure everything is perfectly composed. You can, however, position your subject in the correct part of the frame, and by scanning the scene first for likely distractions you can move so that they are not included in the frame.

Perfect composure

When you frame your subject, you have to balance two requirements. You need to close in as tightly as possible, so that there is no irrelevant background in the shot. But you also need to leave room around the subject in case it moves. You have to judge every shot individually.

Although your subject is likely to be near the middle of the frame, always scan the edges as well. You don't want people or odd bits of building half in and out of the frame. Fortunately, as camcorders have extensive zoom lenses, you can frame your shot very precisely.

If your subject moves, and you move the camcorder to follow it, make sure you keep horizontal lines – especially the horizon itself – level.

Depth and colour

Apart from framing the subject correctly, you should also scan the scene for depth. While your eyes can perceive depth, the TV screen is two dimensional. Forgetting this can lead to classic composition errors, such as lampposts sticking out of the top of people's heads.

Colour is another important factor. Most electronic viewfinders only show a black and white image, so you have to survey the scene with your eyes too.

Look out for two things. First, make sure your main subject stands out from the background – somebody in a green coat shouldn't stand against a green hedge, for instance.

Second, ensure there isn't a distracting splash of colour in the frame that is nothing to do with your main subject. Red is especially attractive to the eye, but bright yellows and oranges also tend to draw attention, so make sure there's no unwanted colour lurking in the background.

▼ ***Aim for a well composed scene. The main subject includes striking colour and the man is off-centre, looking in towards the centre. There are no distractions at the edge of the frame.***

The eyes have it

In the same way that moving subjects generate imaginary lines along the path of their movement, eyes also generate imaginary lines in the direction they are looking.

This is most apparent when two people face each other and an 'eyeline' is created between them. The same rules apply to eyelines as to lines of movement.

When you shoot two or three shots of the couple, pausing the camcorder and changing position between shots, you should remain on one side of the eyeline.

About face

If you cross this eyeline between shots, a person who was facing towards the right appears now to be facing towards the left. The couple seem to have swapped places.

When you shoot two people in this situation, start with an establishing shot that shows both of them. You can then cut to individual close-ups and end by cutting back to the two of them.

from position A

▲ ***Position A. Start with an establishing shot of the couple. From this position you can swap to positions B or C, as they are both on the same side of the line as A.***

from position D

▲ ***Position D. This shot is incorrect – it should not follow an establishing shot from position A. The effects of crossing the line are clear – the girl appears to have swapped positions.***

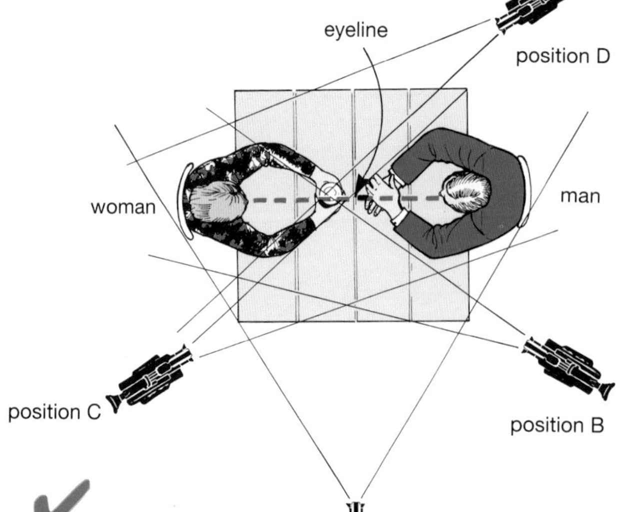

▼ ***Position B. Cut to the person on the left. This shot is a perfectly logical follow-up to the establishing shot, as the person still appears to be looking towards the right.***

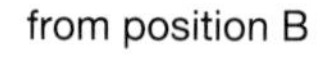

from position B

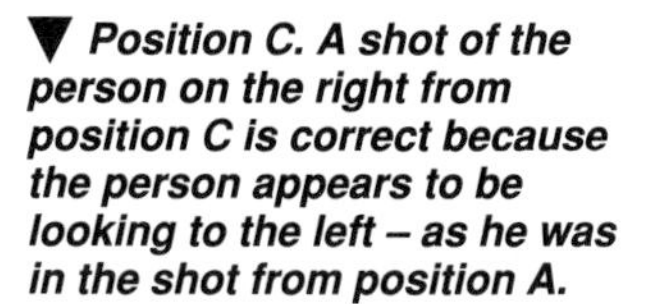

▼ ***Position C. A shot of the person on the right from position C is correct because the person appears to be looking to the left – as he was in the shot from position A.***

from position C

In the frame

You should aim to make the elements in your frame look attractive. It is tempting to place the subject in the centre of the frame, but this is not always the best idea.

Artists and photographers realized years ago that a scene is most pleasing to the eye if the main elements lie a third of the way in from the edge of the frame rather than in the centre.

When you look through your camcorder's viewfinder, imagine the scene divided into thirds, both horizontally and vertically. Try to compose the shot so that the important elements lie on these third lines, rather than in the middle. This is called the 'rule of thirds'.

The four points where the horizontal and vertical third lines meet are the most visually interesting parts of the frame. This makes them the best places to put the most important part of the subject, such as a person's head.

Looking in

When composing close-ups of faces, there are optimum positions for the face to be placed in the frame. When the subject is looking across the frame, particularly if they are walking, make sure there's more room in the direction they are facing or moving than behind them.

Space in front of the subject is called looking (or walking) room. The area behind the head in the frame is 'redundant space', and should be kept to a minimum.

However closely you crop on the face, you should aim to position the eyes about a third of the way down the frame. If the face is positioned lower, the person appears to be falling off the screen.

▲ ***The faces are positioned correctly in the frame with plenty of looking room for the pair to gaze into.***

✗

▲ ***Incorrect positioning. There is too much empty 'redundant space' to the left of the frame.***

✔

▲ ***The subjects are correctly positioned. The eyes are roughly a third of the way from the top of the screen.***

✗

▲ ***Incorrect. The eyes are far too low down, so the people appear to sink off the bottom of the screen.***

Cut-off points

If you video a person in long shot, the entire body is in the frame. As you get closer, be aware of where you cut the person off at the bottom of the frame – like when you take a photo.

Avoid the neck, waist and knees as cut-off points, as this looks odd. If you shoot somebody's head and neck in close-up, without including the person's shoulders, you can give the uncomfortable impression that the person has been decapitated.

Unless you're getting in really close – only including the eyes, nose and mouth – the best cut-off points are level with the armpits, just below the waist and just above the knees.

PROJECT Talking points

It is a lot easier to see how important good composition is with video if you shoot a set sequence and play it back on the TV screen.

The following two sequences cover exactly the same subject matter – a brief conversation between two people – but are shot in two different ways. One places the subject in the correct position in the frame, the other does not.

Ask a couple of friends to join in this exercise. Each sequence is composed of four brief shots, during which the man and the woman each say two sentences. The woman speaks first, then the man, then the woman, and finally the man. It doesn't matter what the people say to each other – the sound isn't important for this exercise.

Shoot the sequence twice from the positions marked in the diagram. When you play back the two sequences, you will notice how the first makes visual sense and the other doesn't.

In the first sequence, all the rules of composition outlined in ths chapter are followed. In the second they are ignored.

Sequence 1
correct sequence

▲ ***Shoot a mid shot of both people from position A, eyes about a third of the way down the screen and torsos cut off above the waist. The woman says her first line.***

▲ ***Close-up of man's head and shoulders from position B as he says his first line. Put him roughly a third of a way in from the left hand edge of the frame, his eyes a third of the way from the top.***

▲ ***Close-up of woman from position C as she says her second line. Place her a third in from the right hand edge, her eyes a third down.***

▲ ***Closing shot from position A, with the same composition as the first shot. The man says his final line.***

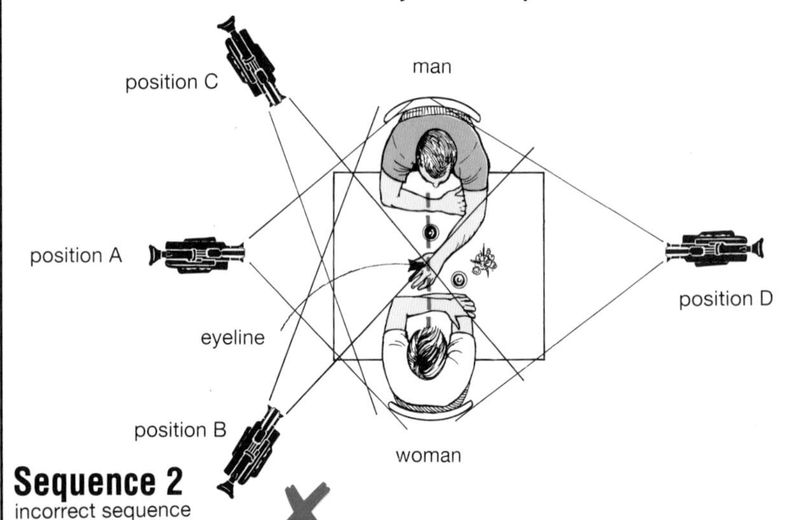

CHECK IT !

Before videoing people, check the following:

❏ **Eyelines** are generated between two people. Take shots from only one side of this line.

❏ **Looking room** Leave some space in the direction the person is looking.

❏ **Cut-off points** Choose them carefully. Don't cut off at the neck – include some shoulder.

❏ **Rule of thirds** Place eyes around a third of the way down from the top of the screen when shooting in close-up.

Sequence 2
incorrect sequence

▲ ***Opening shot the same as the first sequence, taken from position A. The couple are positioned in the correct part of the frame as the man says his first line.***

▲ ***Shot of man from B. Place him a third of the way from the right edge, his eyes half way down the frame, cut off close to the neck. See how he appears to sink.***

▲ ***Shot of woman from C. Place her a third of the way from the left hand edge of the frame. Notice how there is far too much redundant space behind her head.***

▲ ***Final shot from position D of both man and woman. Even correctly composed, notice how the couple appear to have swapped places as the line has been crossed.***

Camera height

Most people hold the camcorder at their own head height when recording, but by shooting from a higher or lower angle you can change the appearance of your subject – and the effect it has on the viewer.

The standard way of shooting a subject is from straight on, with the camcorder held level. This is known as a 'neutral' shot.

Most shots should be recorded with the camcorder level. For people standing, this normally means the camcorder being between 1.5 and 2 metres from the ground.

As most people are of similar height, the natural inclination to video them at chest-to-head height is correct. This is the most comfortable position to hold a camcorder.

Remember, however, that subjects are not always at head height. If someone is sitting down, for instance, you should lower yourself to shoot at their height, which is normally just over a metre above the ground.

There are also subjects that are shorter than adults, such as children and some animals. In order to achieve the same neutral shot, you must lower yourself until you are their height.

Natural view

If your subject is naturally viewed from below or above, then the angle you shoot it from should reflect this. For instance, if you are showing a tall building, shoot it from below with the camera pointing up, as this looks most natural.

In other circumstances you may wish to represent the point of view of one of your subjects. In this case, you should shoot from their head height, regardless of the height of what you are recording.

For instance, if you are videoing a child from an adult's point of view you should shoot down on them, because it is the adult's view you are representing. Similarly, if you are showing an adult from a child's point of view, shoot from below.

▲ ***Under normal circumstances, shoot with the camcorder level. When videoing an adult standing, hold it between head or chest height. This is easier if you and the subject are about the same height.***

◀ ***When somebody is sitting down, you should still hold the camcorder level. This means getting down to their height with the camcorder. Some camcorders have viewfinders that twist up, so you can look down, but it may be steadier if you crouch down.***

◀ ***For babies or toddlers sitting on the ground, lying down gives much more interesting results than shooting from above.***

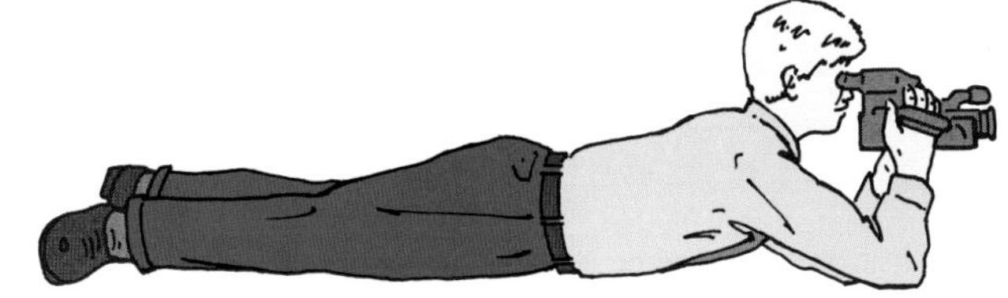

Low point

If you are videoing a subject normally viewed with the camcorder held level, there are two reasons why you might shoot it with the camera tilted up. The first, as mentioned above, is when the shot represents the point of view of somebody looking up; the second is for dramatic effect.

Looking up at a subject makes it appear more prominent, whether it is a person or an object. Statues or sculptures, for instance, look a lot more imposing when shot from below.

People appear more important when seen in mid or long shot from below. If you shoot from only slightly lower than normal, with the camera angled up slightly, the person merely appears very tall.

Lower the camcorder and tilt it up further and they begin to look more powerful – or even threatening. Another interesting effect is that the background appears a lot lower than when the camcorder is held level, so the person also appears to dominate their surroundings.

The psychological explanation for this effect is called 'subject strength/viewer weakness'. If the viewer is looking up at someone, that person appears to be in a position of strength over them.

This technique is very useful when the person is saying something important, as the viewpoint lends authority to the words.

▲ ***If you want to emphasize the power and strength of a subject, shoot them from slightly below. Not only is the American footballer looking down on the audience, giving him the appearance of superiority over them, he also appears taller then the players behind him.***

Portraiture

With people in close-up, the angle you shoot them from can dramatically alter their features. The different effects on your subject's facial appearance is known as portraiture.

Shooting a person from below by 45° or more is not generally complimentary, as facial features tend to be exaggerated.

Looking up at a person can make their nostrils appear unnaturally large, while some people's ears stick out a lot more noticeably than when viewed head on. Men who have receding hairlines can look completely bald, while double chins are given greater prominence.

Videoing from 45° or more above is unkind to balding men, too, as the top of the head is the most prominent feature.

Close-ups from above can also make people look fatter than they are. This is particularly noticeable if you use the wide angle end of the zoom lens.

▲ ***Shots of people from straight on look 'right' because we are used to viewing them in this way. When we change the camera height, however, we can alter their appearance.***

▲ ***Viewing from below draws attention to the man's chin and gives prominence to his nostrils. Be aware of this unflattering effect when you shoot up at someone.***

▲ ***Looking down on this subject draws attention to the top of his head – less desirable if he is losing hair. The eyes are also narrowed, so the man looks as if he is squinting.***

High point

Recording people in long or mid shot from above has the opposite effect of shooting them from below.

If shot from only slightly above, the person merely looks short. If you raise the camera a little higher, they can appear weak or insignificant.

This is based on the principle of 'viewer strength/subject weakness'. By looking down on the subject, the viewer feels in a position of strength, which makes anything the subject says or does appear less important.

Use this technique if you interview somebody and want what they are saying to sound less convincing.

Only the lonely

If you shoot someone from above with a lot of space about them, they can appear isolated and lonely. If you want to show them looking sad, lift the camera above them and shoot down.

High angles can also show somebody who is sorry. If you have somebody apologizing in your video, again shoot them from slightly above.

The effect depends very much on the subject, however, as shooting a scene from above can add a homely feeling to a domestic scene.

◀ ***Videoing from above gives the viewer a sense of superiority over the subject. It is appropriate for scenes where the subject is feeling either depressed or thoughtful. By leaving a lot of room around the boy, you add to the sense of isolation.***

Extreme angles

Extreme high angles are often combined with extreme long shots to provide establishing scenes. A good example of this is a high vista shot looking down on a location. Such long establishers can be either static shots or pans.

People rarely look straight down on to a subject unless they are scrutinizing it – such as when looking down a microscope – or spying on someone without being seen. Extreme low angles can have a similar feel.

High angle shots that look down on to a subject or scene are used in the same way. When the camera shows a view looking down from a high window, the viewer does not feel directly involved in the action, even if it is something dramatic, such as a fight.

Shots looking straight down are often used to show the point of view of someone looking down. In one shot show someone looking out of a window; in the next, show the scene below.

◀ ***The extreme angle distances the viewer from the subject. The audience is placed in the position of spying on the man, rather than being involved in what he is doing.***

▶ ***Looking down on the floor of the New York stock exchange lets us see a large part of the scene, while removing the viewer from the immediate action. By following the shot of the man at the window, this becomes his point of view.***

PROJECT Point of view

When you are faced with a choice of heights at which you can hold the camera – because there are subjects in the scene at different heights – first decide whose point of view you are trying to associate with in the shot.

Hold the camera at around the head height of the person whose point of view you want the audience to relate to.

If you have a person and a dog willing to appear in one of your home videos, shoot the following scene exactly as described. An adult and small child could be used instead if finding a dog presents a difficulty.

In this scene, a dog is creating havoc in the sitting room. The owner appears on the scene and tells the dog off.

In each of these shots choose the camera height of the subject whose point of view you are showing. This is not necessarily the subject of the shot.

◀ DOG FROM DOG'S HEIGHT
To begin the scene, show the dog enjoying itself messing up the sitting room. In order to relate to the dog, shoot from its head height, which is just off the ground.

▼ OWNER FROM DOG'S HEIGHT
The adult enters the room, and the dog anticipates trouble. Show the person from the dog's point of view. Keep the camera at the dog's head level and shoot the person in long to mid shot.

▲ DOG FROM OWNER'S HEIGHT
Show the owner's frustration. Because you are moving sympathy away from the dog, shoot the scene in long shot. Because you are showing how it looks to the owner, shoot from their head height.

▶ OWNER FROM OWNER'S HEIGHT
Finally, you want the viewer to feel sympathy for the owner's frustration, so shoot them from their head height. To reinforce the association, again shoot in close-up.

Tilting and panning

If you can't fit the whole scene in the camcorder's field of view, the answer may be to swing the camcorder while recording by tilting and panning, shots which allow you to follow a moving subject smoothly.

There are several ways of exploring a scene or scenes. One is to move your position and reframe the shot. Another is to stay where you are and zoom in or out.

You can also use moving shots – two of the more common are pans and tilts. Panning involves swinging the camcorder in a smooth arc from left to right or right to left. Tilting is tipping the camcorder smoothly up or down.

There are two main uses for either shot. One is to follow a subject that is moving, at a consistent speed. The other is so that the whole of a scene can be shown without the need to cut from detail to detail.

This is a good way of linking two subjects that are in the same location, but some way apart. If you want to change from one to the other, panning round or tilting up or down achieves this while explaining exactly how they relate to each other.

If used to show tall or panoramic scenes, the shots should always end on an interesting subject, which forms the basis of the next shot. Pans or tilts that end in nothing leave the viewer feeling dissatisfied.

When to tilt

Tilts can be used to follow a moving subject, for instance someone diving off a diving board or something falling from a tall building. But they are more commonly used to show a scene that will not fit in a single static shot, or to emphasize the size of the subject.

You can produce a comic or dramatic effect by shooting a tilt shot of a person, starting from a low angle pointing at their feet and slowly tilting up until you reach the head. This conveys that the figure is very tall or very threatening, or both.

Ensure the camcorder is level with the ground by keeping horizontal lines in your viewfinder parallel to the bottom of your frame. (With the constant changes of perspective, vertical lines appear diagonal and are less useful as visual clues.)

Getting a smooth tilt

Tilts must be smooth and steady. Jerky movements look amateurish and should be avoided at all costs.

The best way to avoid jerkiness is to use a tripod, but as this is not always possible practise tilting while handholding the camcorder. To get the smoothest tilt, plant your feet about half a metre apart, facing slightly out, and move your body from your waist, not your neck. This gives the smoothest movement.

Practise a few times to get it right before you start recording, and don't start to move as soon as you go into record mode. Hold the shot for a short while before beginning to move, and similarly hold the end shot for a few seconds. This allows for the camcorder's backspace time before it begins recording, and it looks better than immediately launching into camera movement. It also gives you the flexibility to cut at the right point if you want to edit the video afterwards.

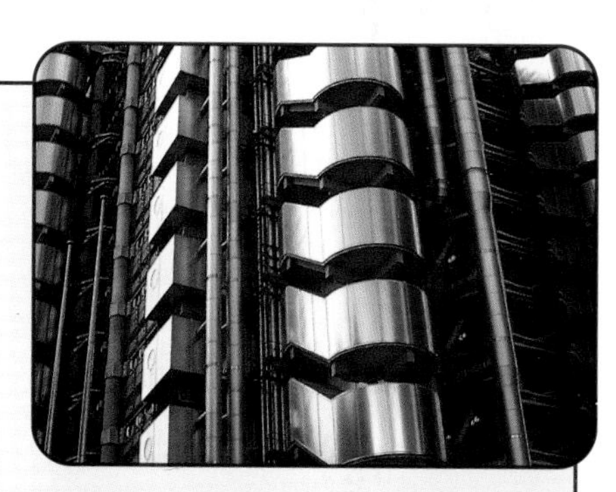

▶ ***Tall buildings provide perfect subjects for tilts. Start at the top and slowly tilt down until you get to the entrance. This is an interesting way of establishing the location and leads in easily to the next scene, which could be of somebody coming out of the building or one of the inside of the foyer.***

Perfect panning

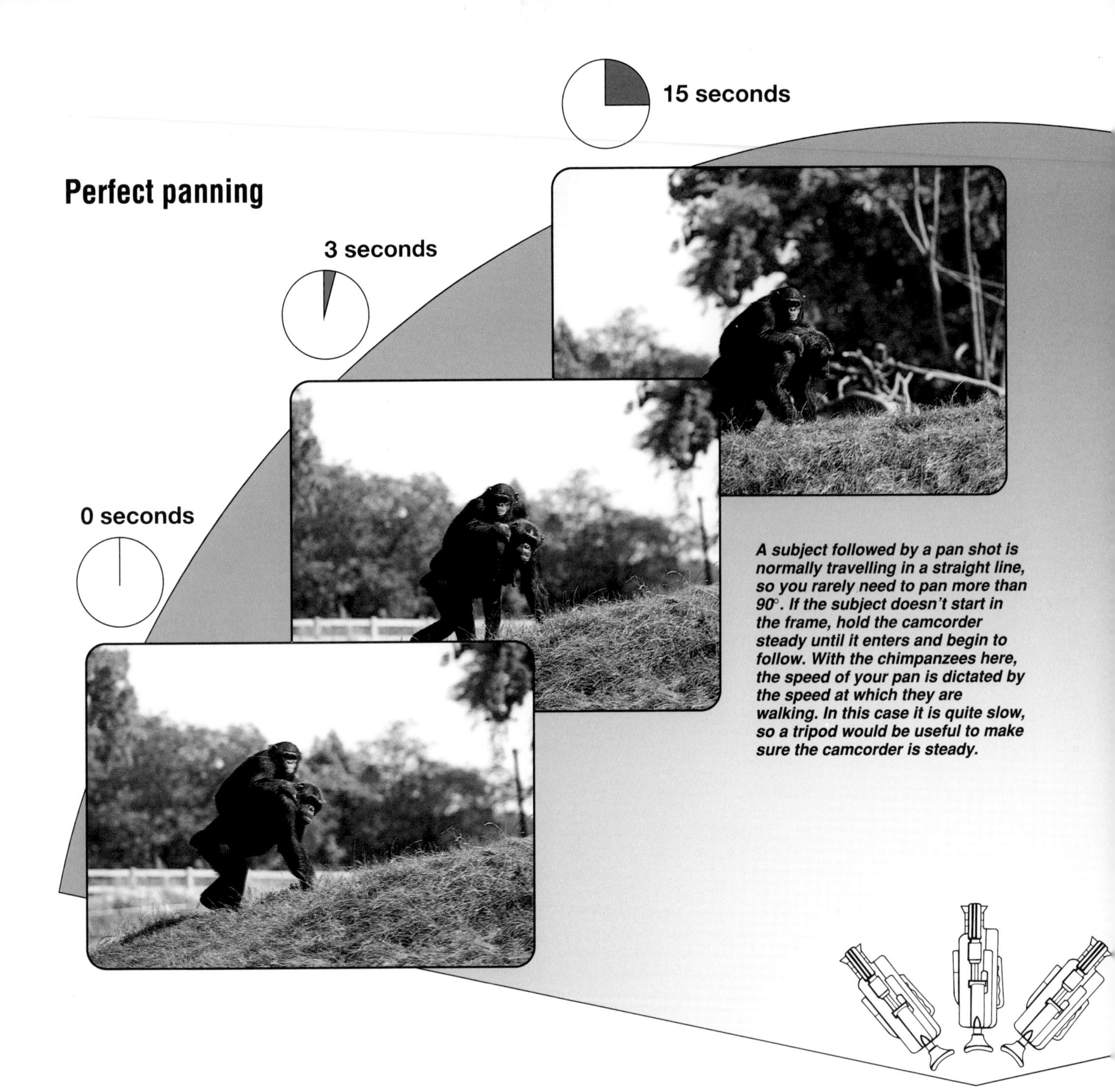

A subject followed by a pan shot is normally travelling in a straight line, so you rarely need to pan more than 90°. If the subject doesn't start in the frame, hold the camcorder steady until it enters and begin to follow. With the chimpanzees here, the speed of your pan is dictated by the speed at which they are walking. In this case it is quite slow, so a tripod would be useful to make sure the camcorder is steady.

Avoid hosepiping

As with zoom shots, the most important thing to remember about panning is not to overuse the technique. If you pan to the left and then to the right as if you were watering a flowerbed, you bewilder the viewer. This misuse of the pan is called 'hosepiping' and often happens when you're not sure what the main subject is. Plan your scene first so you're quite clear what you want to record.

Panning is an effective but often misused technique. By swinging the camcorder in a horizontal arc, you can follow a moving subject or take in a vast panorama.

Panning from one view to another allows you to see how two or more objects or groups of people relate to each other and enables you to direct the viewer's attention from one subject to another.

Panning, like tilting, should be a smooth movement. If you are not using a tripod or any other form of support, stand with your feet firmly apart and swing from your hips, rather than your shoulders.

The pan should have a definite beginning and end – as with tilting, hold the start and end shots for a few seconds, as if they were normal static shots.

The smoothest action comes when you twist your body. Position yourself so that you are facing the final point of your pan, and move smoothly in the direction you wish to pan from. When you have gone through 90° and are facing to the side, your body will be tensed. From this position you can pan slowly back until you face the front again.

Although you might be able to stretch yourself further, the human body can only comfortably pan through about 90° while holding the camcorder steady.

Getting the speed right

Practise panning and playing back the results. Many people at first fall into a common trap of panning too fast – it can seem as though you're taking ages to record, but once on screen you appear to be scudding across the action!

Again, ensure the bottom of the screen is parallel to any horizontal lines in your scene. Vertical lines, such as telegraph poles and the sides of buildings, should be parallel to the edge of the frame.

If you are editing later, you can start recording before you begin the pan, and edit out that part afterwards. Otherwise, start recording as soon as you get to the start position.

If you are following a fast-moving subject, your pace is determined by the speed at which it is travelling. Frame the subject so that it lags slightly behind the centre of the picture – this is called giving the subject 'moving room'.

As with tilts you can combine panning with zooming, particularly when following a moving subject.

If you zoom in on a subject that is moving, it might move out of the frame if you keep your camcorder stationary. With electronic zooms, you can zoom in on a subject while panning.

If you plan it right, by the time you reach the end of your pan, you also reach the end of your zoom, with the back of the subject slowly fading into the distance.

Tripods with fluid heads

One way of ensuring your pans and tilts are smooth is to use a tripod with a fluid head.

Use a tripod that's for camcorders, not stills cameras. A stills camera tripod is designed to keep the camera steady when you press the shutter. The head is not intended for mobility and is therefore not suitable for pan and tilt shots.

Camcorder tripod heads are designed with pans and tilts in mind. Expensive tripods have genuine 'fluid' heads – the top of the head floats on a layer of liquid, ensuring ultra-smooth movement.

'Fluid-effect' heads are cheaper and give similar smooth pans by resting on ball bearings. The whole purpose of fluid heads is to achieve smooth movement by cutting down on friction. Some fluid heads cut friction to almost zero, so that the head continues to move on its own after an initial push.

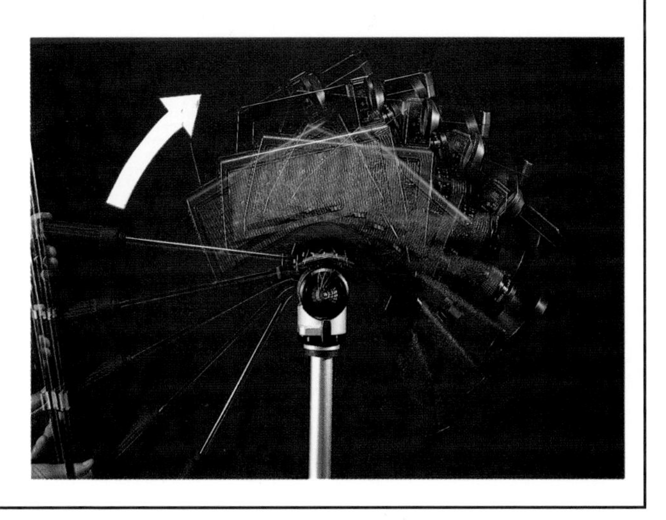

PROJECT On safari

Safari parks provide excellent locations for trying out panning and tilting.

Combine your knowledge of long shots, mid shots and close-ups with what you know about panning and tilting to produce a short film of an outing to a safari park.

A good opening might be a pan shot that begins with a static shot of a car coming into view. As the car turns into the entrance of the safari park, pan round to follow it.

Cut to a close-up of the sign giving the name of the park. Another opening might be somebody looking at a map or guidebook. There may be other opportunities later to pan round to take in the panoramic location.

Use a lot of short static shots of different animals near the beginning of the video to show the extent of the wildlife collection. Apart from conveying a lot of information, this will contrast with the slower pan and tilt shots.

If you get close enough to a giraffe, you have an opportunity to use a tilt shot to emphasize the creature's height.

The closer you are, the more acute the tilt. Tilt very slowly up or down the neck. If you go too quickly, the shot is over in a second and you lose all the impact.

You don't want to overdo your pans and tilts, but one way of ending the video might be to use the same pan idea as you started the video with, only this time having the car drive away into the distance.

▲ ***You can combine the tilt with a zoom towards the end of the shot, so that you fill the frame with the giraffe's head. Otherwise it might look a bit lost against the background, and this device reduces any problem with backlighting.***

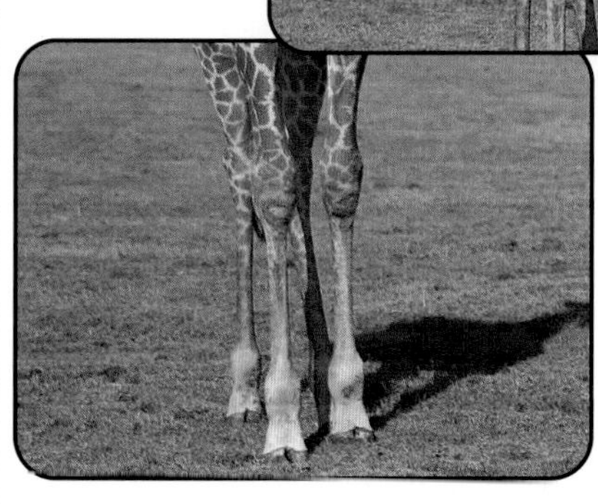

▶ ***Giraffes are an ideal subject for tilting. Try moving slowly up the legs, body and neck to finish on the creature's head.***

CHECK IT!

When panning or tilting

- ❑ If using the shot to reveal detail about a location, end on something interesting. The action could then move to that subject.
- ❑ Review your pan or tilt after you've shot it. If it's jerky, do it again where possible.
- ❑ Look out for horizontal and vertical straight lines in your scene to use as guidelines for holding the camcorder level.
- ❑ Hold the start of the pan for a few seconds before you begin to move. This gives the viewer time to take in the location.
- ❑ If you are hand holding your camcorder while panning, end the pan facing forward.
- ❑ Don't devalue these two shots by overuse.

The moving camera

Professional TV and movie directors often use tracking shots – where the camera moves while recording. Such shots can look impressive, but you have to take precautions to make sure the movement is smooth.

So far, the only shots we have looked at are those where the camera operator stays in one place while recording. Even when you move your camcorder for pan and tilt shots, your feet should remain firmly rooted in one spot.

There is nothing wrong with moving the camera while recording, but such 'tracking' shots can be difficult to execute without the expensive equipment available to the professional. If the camcorder wobbles during a moving camera shot, the viewer notices the shot and not the subject.

Tracking shots can be used to move towards or away from a stationary subject. You can move from long shot to close-up without having to pause the camcorder.

In this way they are similar to zoom shots, but the effect is more natural, because the perspective change imitates the experience of movement. Zooming, on the other hand, looks unnatural.

Dramatic tension

When the subject matter is intimate, cutting can be obtrusive, and a gentle move towards a person or couple can work a lot better. Similarly, when the action is highly dramatic, moving closer produces a build-up of tension, such as when the camera rushes towards someone at a moment of realization.

Moving out from a subject gives importance to the surroundings. The effect is to slowly reveal the location – emphasizing its importance. Again, a zoom out is a poor compromise because it doesn't give the same sense of moving away.

Moving out can be used for humorous or dramatic effect when there is something unexpected in the surroundings. For instance, we move back from somebody waking up to find that someone is in bed with them. Or in a horror movie, we pull back from someone's face to show they are chained up.

▲ Although the subject of this sequence is a girl juggling, it is the girl's face that is the centre of attention, not the juggling balls. The start of the shot shows the girl in mid to long shot, and introduces the subject.

◀▼ As we move in, we direct the viewer's attention to the girl's mental concentration and physical effort. This is shown in her facial expression, not in her arm movements. The move-in helps to build a viewer/subject association.

Power moves

When the camera moves towards a person, it reinforces their power and authority – such as shots where the camera moves towards a hero in a movie. This can be heightened by using a low camera height. From a distance, the camera is almost level, but as you move closer, you have to tilt up the camcorder.

Exploring space

Tracking shots are much better than pans at exploring a location because you can examine details of a scene that a pan shot would miss. You can also show the scene from more than one viewpoint in the same shot.

If you want to show a large space in one shot, pans have the advantage that you can sweep from horizon to horizon in only a few seconds. The disadvantage is that much of the shot is so far away that little detail can be made out.

With a tracking shot, you can explore a scene while keeping all of it fairly close. You are able to show detail throughout the shot. This is also true if you are tracking to follow a moving subject.

For instance, if you use a pan shot to record a couple walking along a path, they start off very small, grow very large in the frame

Using a dolly

▲ ***A tripod dolly – or spider – allows you to track smoothly over a level surface. The spider has a dolly mode, where the casters are down, and a park mode, where the casters are lifted to prevent movement.***

Professionals shoot tracking shots by laying down a mini railway track and pushing the camera along on a wheeled platform, known as a 'dolly'. This is not usually a practical option for the camcorder user, but alternatives are available.

The simplest is a tripod dolly – also called a spider – a set of wheels that connects to the bottom of a tripod to make it mobile. On smooth surfaces, a tripod dolly works fine, but it is difficult to control exposure and focusing while moving the dolly.

Anything with wheels can be used as a dolly, including wheelchairs, cars (so long as the car moves smoothly), or an old fashioned pram: the bigger the wheels, the steadier the track. Or make a dolly from a sturdy bit of wood and four casters.

Better still is the Steadicam JR, a recent innovation. The Steadicam uses a number of weights and counter-balances, as well as a harness, to enable you to move smoothly, while keeping the camcorder steady.

The Steadicam is not cheap, but it does include a mono LCD monitor so you can see what the camcorder is recording without having to put it to your eye. It has the advantage of enabling you to shoot smooth moving shots on uneven ground.

Whatever method you use, try to keep the camcorder on or near its wide angle setting. Slight camera movements are exaggerated when you use the telephoto end.

Cross lines

Moving with the camera allows you to cross the line of action without confusing the viewer. We saw in another chapter that if in one shot you show a person or object moving to the left of the frame, you should not show them looking to the right of the screen in the next shot.

Similarly, if someone is facing in one direction, you should not have them facing in the opposite direction in the next shot. Tracking with the camcorder gets round this problem. If you want to show the subject from both sides, you can simply move with the camcorder from one side to the other. As there is no cut, there is no possibility of confusion.

as they get closer to you, and grow smaller again as they move away.

With a tracking shot, so long as you are moving parallel to the couple and at the same time, the composition of the subject is identical throughout the shot. The only thing that changes is the background.

This allows you to choose the shot size and camera angle you want – as you would for a static shot. You also have the option of either panning at the end of the important action or conversation, or stopping the camera and letting the couple walk out of the frame.

▲ ***By tracking along this row of stalls, rather than panning, we can see each one in detail. Sound is important, too, as we should be able to hear the various conversations as we pass each stall. By using one shot, instead of cutting, the whole market becomes the subject of the shot.***

Crabbing

Normally, you should avoid walking with the camera while recording, as the results can be very unsteady. But in some circumstances there is no alternative.

If you are going to walk with the camcorder, there is a special way of walking that keeps the camcorder steadiest. It is called 'crabbing'.

When you crab, you walk sideways, rather than forwards. If you want to crab to the left, bring your right leg in front of your left leg, so that the back of the right knee touches the front of the left.

By the time your right leg touches the floor, all of your weight has been transferred to your right foot. This means you can bring your left leg round the back of your right without the normal jerkiness that takes place when you transfer your weight from foot to foot walking forwards.

▶ ***To crab, bring one leg in front of the other. At the same time transfer your body weight in the direction you are moving. By the time the foot hits the ground, it should be carrying all the weight. Bring the other foot round the back and repeat the manoeuvre.***

PROJECT Arcing

Another interesting type of shot that moving the camera allows is the arc shot. Arcing is simply moving the camera in a circle or arc instead of a straight line.

Normally, an arc shot is used either to show a subject from all angles or to track round a group of subjects. Either way, the effect of an arc shot is to unify whatever is within the arc and exclude subjects that fall outside it.

Thus, when you arc round a single subject, the shot serves to heighten its importance by isolating it from the rest of its environment. Similarly, when the camera arcs round a group of people, such as diners at a table, a sports or business team, or a group of musicians, it emphasizes the identity of the group, rather than that of the individuals.

Arcing can also make an interesting alternative to simply shooting a static shot of a non-moving subject. If your subject is inanimate – say, a fountain or statue – you can get a far more dynamic and interesting image if you move round it, rather than stand in one spot.

This exploits the natural advantage of continuous movement that a camcorder has over a stills camera. To make the shot as smooth as possible, try to keep the subject at the same position in the frame – normally the centre.

Crab in an arc

Practise crabbing in an arc around a stationary subject to see how much more interesting it looks than if you record it with a straight-forward static shot. The arc should cover between 120° and 180°, with the same part of the subject being in the centre of the frame for the entire movement.

Step by step

1 Choose a small subject, such as a person or couple or a small statue, that you can crab round easily.

2 Get into position for the start of the shot, composing the subject in the centre of the frame.

3 Press the RECORD button and after a few seconds start crabbing, holding the camcorder as steadily as you possibly can. You can move clockwise or anti-clockwise, but anti-clockwise tends to look best, as left to right movements look more natural.

4 Crab slowly and smoothly, keeping the subject at the same position in the frame throughout the shot.

5 When you reach the end position, stop crabbing and hold the shot for a few seconds before pausing.

Sound sense

Recording pictures on your camcorder is only half the story. All camcorders have microphones built in, and both sound and vision are recorded when you start the tape running.

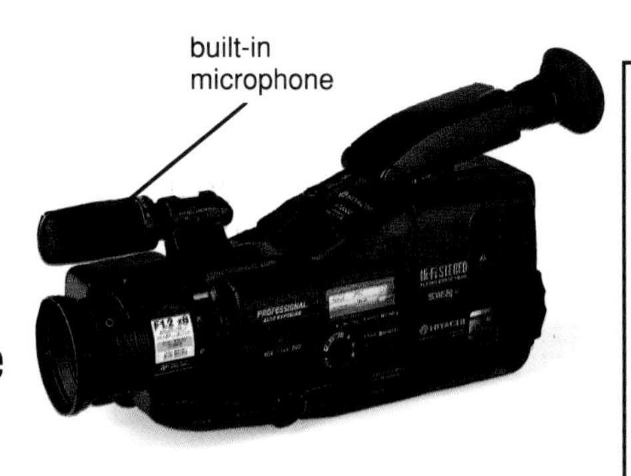
built-in microphone

Psychologists refer to a human attribute called the 'cocktail party phenomenon'. This is the ability of the brain to make out individual conversations or sounds from a babel of background noise.

Whenever you concentrate on a particular sound, the brain very efficiently 'turns down' other audio signals, so that you can listen in relative comfort.

A camcorder doesn't have this ability. So if you want to make a video with a good quality soundtrack, you have to 'relearn' how to listen. You have to be able to hear what the camcorder hears.

Try closing your eyes and listening. Maybe you can hear a fan or heater humming away? Or the noise of distant traffic? Maybe your next door neighbour is out using a lawnmower?

It's surprising the number of sounds you hear but mentally switch off from. When you concentrate you can hear them all. The camcorder doesn't need to concentrate. Check for background noise before you start shooting. When possible, be prepared to shoot again if, say, you are interrupted by a pile-driver starting up.

Finding your level

To gain an idea of how sensitive your microphone is, ask someone to stand at various distances from the camcorder, talking at normal volume.

Play back through your TV and make a note of where you start to lose some of the voice. Try this with two or three people to get a clear idea of how far away you need to stand when you're shooting for real.

If you are recording people talking naturally, say at a party or wedding, you have to listen carefully to what is being said to give you a cue as to when to cut.

Stop recording at a natural break in the conversation, not in the middle of somebody speaking. And if somebody is telling a story or a joke, don't cut them off before they reach the punch line.

Sound and vision

For the clearest sound, record from as close to your subject as possible. The camcorder's extensive zoom range comes to your aid. Setting the lens to the wide angle enables you to move close enough to your subject to get good quality sound, while still keeping in a bit of background.

It's always tempting to use the telephoto and stand well back, as this avoids the problem of people being embarrassed by the camcorder. But it's better to try putting the subjects at their ease than risk losing their conversation.

The art of conversation

A common scene in any movie is two people talking. If you look at how a conversation is shot, you will notice the classic way of shooting this – mingling mid shots that include both participants with close-ups of the people's faces.

Although it's slightly unorthodox, a simpler way of recording a conversation (particularly if it's candid) is to start with a long to mid shot and zoom in to whoever's talking. You can then pan round to the next speaker, or pan round to catch reactions if one person in particular is holding the floor.

You will have to break the rules against panning backwards and forwards, but if you do it slowly and discreetly, it won't be too obtrusive. If there is a general reaction, you can zoom out again.

By standing in the same place, close to your subjects, you ensure that the sound is recorded at an even level.

Opening shot.

Zoom in and pan from one close-up to another.

Shooting out

Shooting outdoors can pose great difficulties for sound recording, as you have very little control over the background noise.

It's no joke when a shot that's going perfectly well is spoiled by the sound of a siren as an ambulance hurtles past. If the noise drowns out your desired soundtrack, there may be nothing for it but to rewind and start the shot again. Even if you're not directing the action you can usually ask people to go through it again.

Because of the general level of noise outdoors, any quiet speaking is lost. Ask the people you're videoing to talk loudly and clearly.

▲ ***The level of wind noise rises and falls rapidly. To combat this it's best to try and block wind interference completely. In this case the wind block is a golfing umbrella placed on the windward side of the camera operator.***

Gone with the wind

One of the major problems of shooting outdoors is wind. Some manufacturers have tried to overcome this by including a 'wind' button on their built-in microphone, which mutes the audio frequencies at which wind operates.

When there is a strong wind blowing, it is worth using a wind block even if you have a wind-mute switch. The block could be a large piece of card or an umbrella held between the wind and the camcorder.

At a push, you can get somebody to use their body to block the wind. If you don't have anyone to help, make use of any natural windbreaks, such as a tree or hedge.

It may be that you're videoing an outdoor event, such as a procession or carnival. In this case it's the overall sound you want to capture, not individual conversations. You should therefore manoeuvre slightly away from other spectators if possible, so that you get a consistent soundtrack.

Get into the habit of standing still, closing your eyes and listening to the background noise before you record every shot. This way you can notice any potentially distracting sounds.

Listening in

A number of camcorders on the market have headphone sockets. By plugging in headphones, you can monitor the sound the microphone is recording.

This is extremely useful, as you are aware of which sounds are registering and which are not. Far less concentration is required to monitor the sound when you use headphones than when you don't.

To get the full advantage, use headphones that fully cover your ears, so you don't have any direct sound interfering.

You can also monitor what you've already recorded when you're wearing headphones. This enables you to check if there are any problems with the sound and gives you the opportunity to re-record a bad take immediately.

Jumping jive

You have to be careful that the sound doesn't jump between cuts. This can occur at a disco or party, where there is music playing in the background. Every time you cut to another shot, the music jumps.

This can be corrected by editing as you become more advanced. But if you don't intend to edit, there's another way round it. Record a shot in the room where the music is playing and follow it by one in another room. If you then cut back, there is no jump.

Shooting in

Although there is less likelihood of being interrupted by stray sounds when you're shooting indoors, a relatively quiet surrounding can give rise to difficulties of its own.

This is because camcorders don't record sound at a constant level. A very small number of top-end machines allow you to alter the recording level manually, but most rely on AGC (automatic gain control).

The AGC automatically increases the recording level when there is little sound and decreases it when there is a lot of noise.

Noises off

If you shoot in a quiet environment, the gain is switched right up, so the camcorder is far more likely to record operating noise, such as the power zoom working or even the operator breathing.

Be especially careful about knocking the body of the camcorder under these circumstances, as the noise would be picked up by the microphone.

Hear no evil

If you are shooting inside your home, there may be certain sounds you are so familiar with you no longer notice them. If you live near a train line or air route, you may switch off to the sound of trains or airplanes. But you must be aware of them so that they don't impose on your video. Pause and continue recording after they have gone by.

Some household appliances, such as freezers, make noises you may no longer hear. Turn them off for a couple of minutes or shoot away from them.

Dead or alive

Recorded sound comes either directly from the subject or is reflected from nearby surfaces. The mix of the two contributes greatly to the type of sound (acoustic environment) produced. Some surfaces are highly reflective, giving a harsh, echoing sound. Such areas are known as acoustically 'alive'. Other surfaces are acoustically 'dead'. They absorb sound, giving a warmer, but muted feel.

Carpets, curtains, sofas and wall-hangings all absorb sound. This makes living rooms particularly suited to cozy, family videos.

If your subject matter is harsh or grim, a reflective acoustic environment may be better suited to it.

Documentaries showing poor living conditions or dramas involving interrogation are usually recorded in rooms with highly reflective surfaces, such as walls, stone floors and windows.

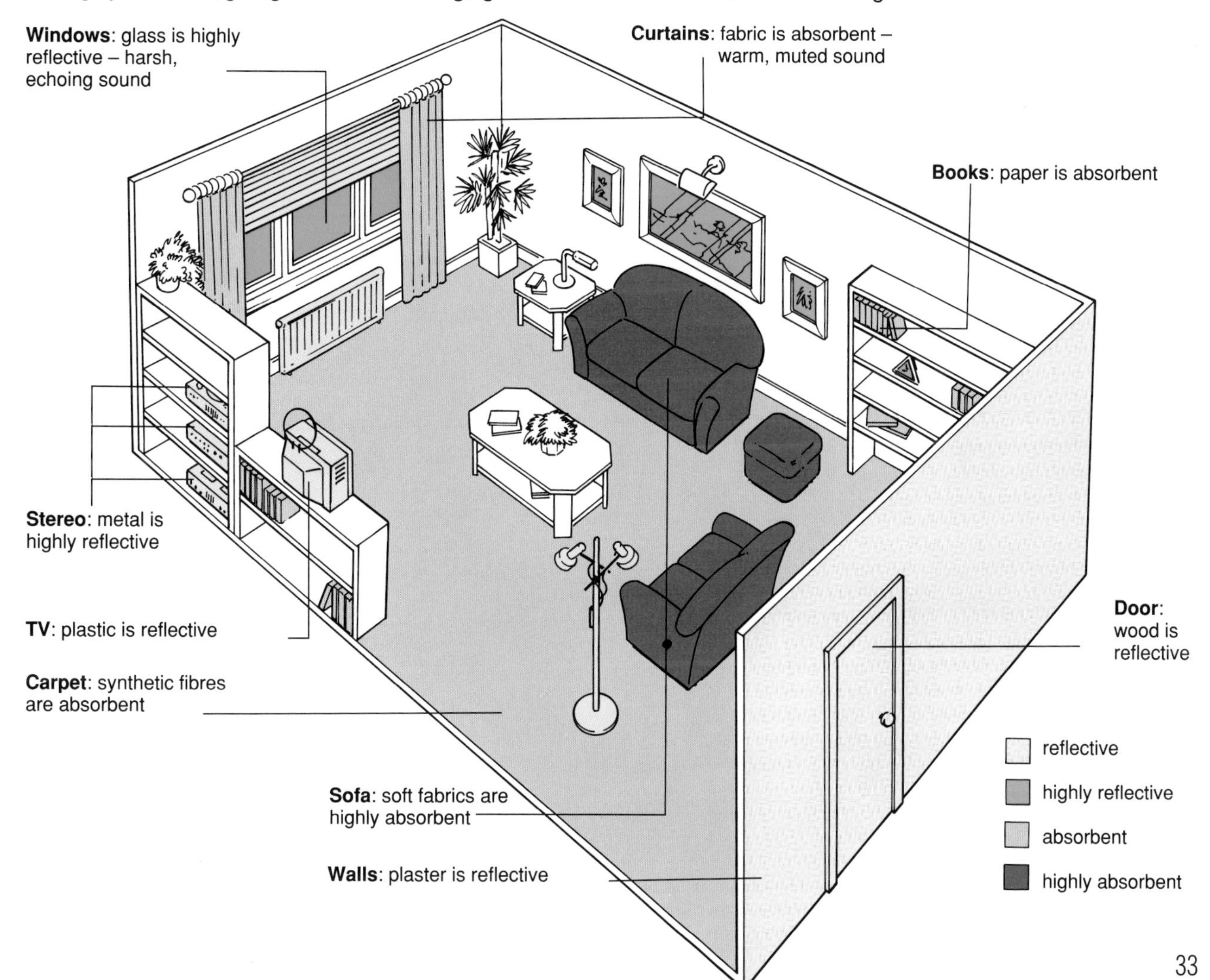

Sound systems

Not all camcorders feature the same sound recording system. There are currently five different systems, each with their own characteristics:

NAME	FOUND ON	GOOD POINTS	BAD POINTS
VHS linear mono	Basic VHS and VHS-C, as well as some older S-VHS machines	Cheap. Recorded on separate part ('track') of the tape to the picture, so it can be re-recorded without affecting picture	Not as good quality as hi-fi recording
8mm FM mono	Budget 8mm camcorders	More space on tape is allotted to sound recording than on linear mono. This leads to more information being recorded and so to better sound quality	Can't change or add to the soundtrack without recording over the picture
VHS hi-fi stereo	S-VHS, S-VHS-C and top end VHS and VHS-C models	Hi-fi recording and stereo give better sound quality than mono systems. Also has a linear mono track, so you can dub new sound on this part of the tape, mixing it with the picture and the original sound, which is recorded on the left and right stereo hi-fi tracks	Slightly more expensive. Added sound on the linear track is of lower quality than sound on the hi-fi track
FM/AFM stereo (two different but similar systems)	Hi8 and top-end 8mm camcorders	Records in stereo on two hi-fi tracks (left and right). Gives better sound quality than mono systems	More expensive than mono recording. Again, can't record over sound without recording over picture
PCM stereo	Semi-professional models	Used as an addition to FM/AFM stereo. It is an exceptionally high quality system and can be audio dubbed without affecting the picture	Expensive

Audio dubbing

With VHS mono linear recording, the sound is recorded in a different place or track on the tape from the picture. This means that, so long as your camcorder has an audio dub function, you can re-record the sound afterwards without affecting the picture.

On most 8mm or Hi8 camcorders, you can't audio dub because the sound is in the same position on the tape as the picture. This means that if you redub the sound, you record over the picture.

VHS hi-fi stereo camcorders feature a left and right hi-fi track, which are recorded in the same place as the picture, as well as a mono linear recording track, so you can audio dub with these too. On hi-fi stereo machines, you can add new sound to the mono track without recording over the original sound on the hi-fi tracks.

Another way of audio dubbing with VHS and VHS-C is to transfer the tape from the camcorder to a video recorder with audio dub facility (in the case of VHS-C via an adapter) and record new sound through an add-on microphone or from a tape recorder.

With the audio dub function, you can add commentary by talking into either the camcorder's microphone or the add-on mic plugged into the video recorder's mic-in socket, though the original sound is lost.

PCM sound also offers audio dub facility, but gives far superior quality because it records the information digitally, like a compact disc. This eliminates any background hiss or interference. However, a camcorder equipped with PCM is very expensive.

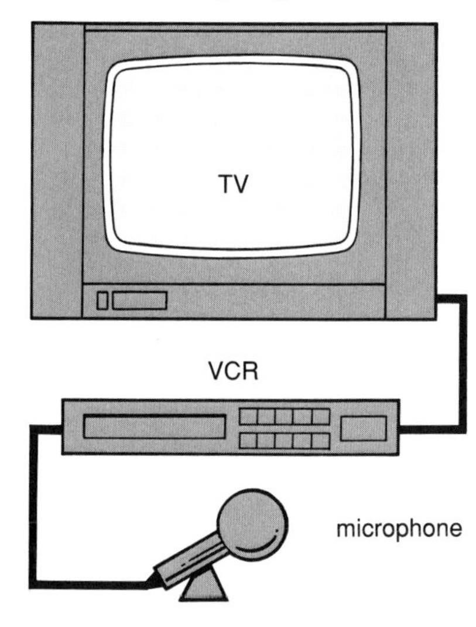

Advanced sound techniques

Once you have mastered the art of recording sound properly with your camcorder, you are ready to move on to more advanced techniques.

All camcorders have built-in microphones, but separate add-on mics, placed next to the subject, are often more appropriate.

For instance, if you are recording a conversation outdoors, it may be marred by background noise. Unless you stand very close to your subject, the camcorder's mic will not pick up the words clearly.

An accessory mic, placed close to the subject, allows you to move the camcorder further away from the speaker. This lets you include the location without compromising the sound.

A microphone close to the speakers picks up the conversation and blocks out the unwanted background noise.

As it is not mounted on the camcorder, there is no danger of the camcorder's operating noise (such as the buzz of the autofocus system or power zoom) being recorded on the soundtrack.

Add-on mics come in specialized varieties, so you can choose the most appropriate one for your shooting needs.

Constant sound

Another advantage of using a separate mic is that it frees the camcorder to move around without affecting the sound.

Imagine following a guided tour in a museum. You can get somebody else to hold the mic next to the tour guide so that you catch everything being said. Meanwhile, the camcorder can take in the various exhibits.

The person with the microphone has to stay fairly close to the camcorder, otherwise there is a danger of people becoming entangled in the wire.

Some camcorders have an external shoe to which you can fit an add-on mic. However, extra mics are normally plugged into the camcorder's mic socket and placed off the camcorder.

Tip: Wired for sound

For recording speech, clip-on omnidirectional mics are a good option, so long as the person wearing them doesn't knock them, as this produces sound interference.

Wireless mics are available. These come in two parts – transmitter (which clips on to clothing) and receiver (which attaches to the camcorder).

If you are recording from far enough away, the radio mic will be invisible. This allows you to shoot long shots, while recording sound as if you were standing much closer to the speaker.

Mic types

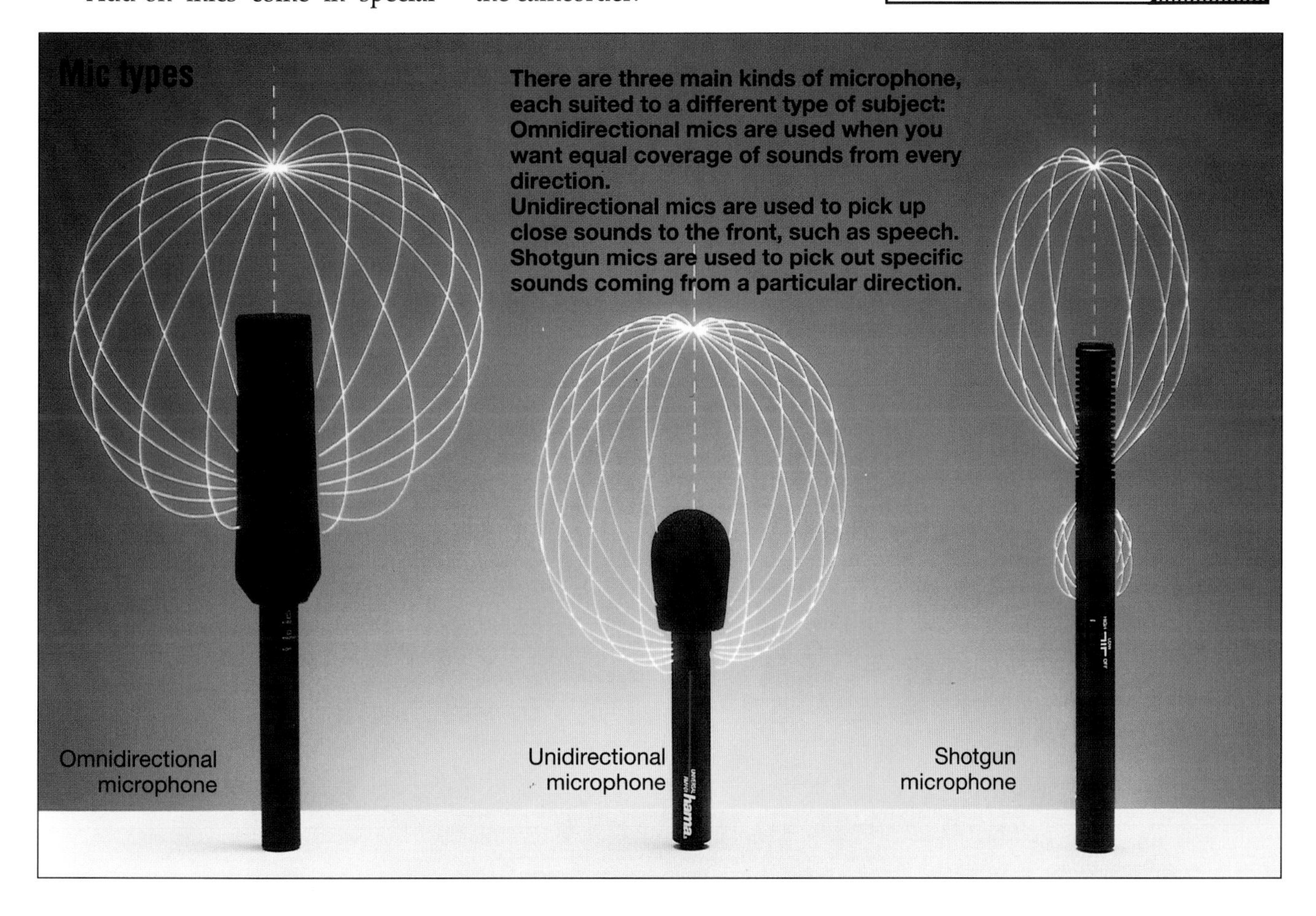

There are three main kinds of microphone, each suited to a different type of subject: Omnidirectional mics are used when you want equal coverage of sounds from every direction. Unidirectional mics are used to pick up close sounds to the front, such as speech. Shotgun mics are used to pick out specific sounds coming from a particular direction.

Omnidirectional microphone

Unidirectional microphone

Shotgun microphone

Sound assistance

You could ask a friend to be your sound assistant when you are out videoing. With a second person looking after sound, you're free to concentrate on composing the shots.

At the most basic level, the sound assistant just holds the extension mic in position. A useful accessory for an assistant is a boom – a long stick to which a mic is attached. The sound assistant holds the boom over the heads of the people talking, just out of shot.

The sound quality is far superior to recording with the camcorder's built-in microphone. However, if you are recording outside using the built-in mic, the assistant can also hold a windshield to cut out any excess wind noise.

Separate sound

The ideal way to record sound – and the way the professionals do it – is to use separate sound recording equipment and mix the sound and picture together while editing.

If you have a good assistant – and the appropriate equipment – you can leave the sound recording to them. You can still follow the sound, but your assistant can concentrate solely on monitoring the recording level and letting you know when background noise becomes obtrusive. They must wear headphones.

▲ A sound assistant can hold the microphone above or below the speakers on a boom. Both mic and assistant are out of shot. Here the boom is improvised, made out of a broom handle with the mic tied to the end with string.

Sound devices

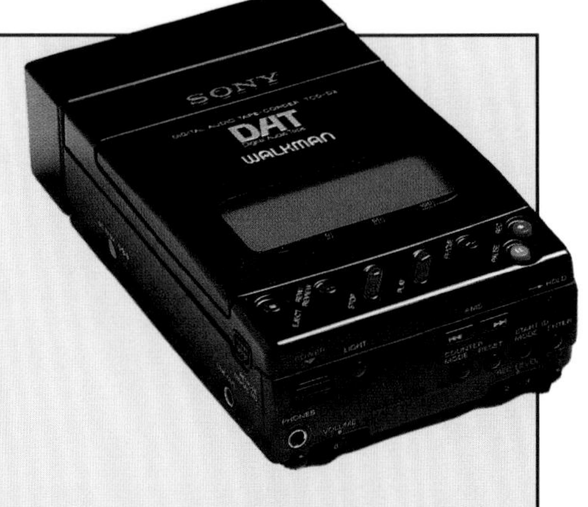

The simplest sound recording set up consists of a microphone, a portable tape recorder and a pair of headphones to monitor the sound.

If possible, use a recorder with manual recording levels, so you can alter it to suit the conditions. If your recorder has manual recording levels, it may also have a VU meter built in, with a needle that indicates the sound level. You have to keep this needle out of the red area, otherwise the sound distorts.

If the recording level is too low, you may get background hiss on the soundtrack, only some of which can be eliminated with Dolby noise reduction.

This hiss is inherent in conventional audio recording. However, it is eliminated in digital recording formats such as DAT (digital audio tape) and DCC (digital compact cassette). On the down side, digital sound equipment can be a lot more expensive than conventional tape recorders. If you are using a standard tape recorder, the quality of the tape you use can make a big difference. Metal and chrome tapes give better sound reproduction than standard ferric cassettes. Although they are slightly more expensive, the extra cost is comparatively small.

A good mix

In some Hollywood movies, as little as 10% of the soundtrack is recorded at the same time as the picture. Commentary, sound effects and music are all added at a later date, and you even get the chance to overdub if you lose part of the original dialogue.

While you don't need to be as advanced with home recordings, adding extra sound can enhance your video. The various elements are mixed together at the editing stage using a sound mixer. Basic sound mixers are cheap and easy to use.

To make use of a sound mixer, you need to use a video recorder with separate audio and video inputs. This is because the video output from the camcorder connects straight to the video input on the video recorder. Only the audio output from the camcorder has to connect to the audio mixer.

Sound set-up

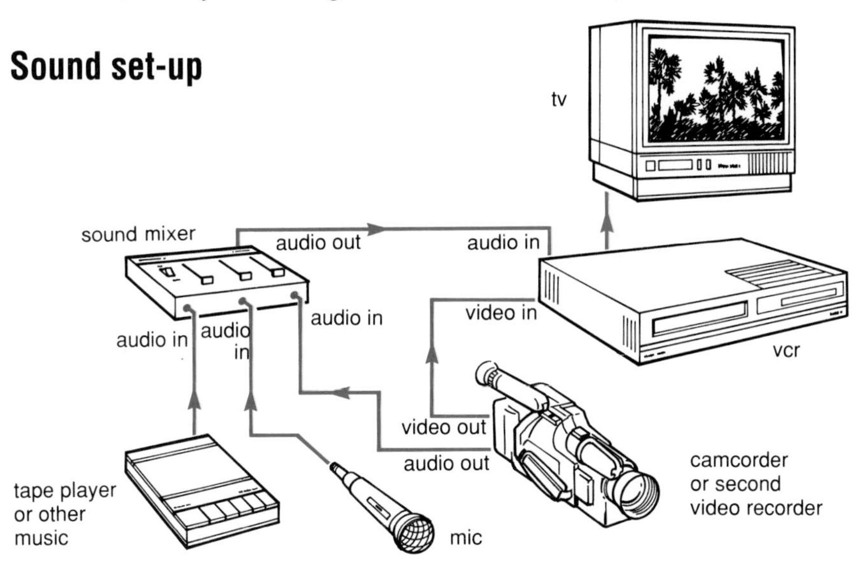

◀ Connect the audio output from the camcorder to one of the audio inputs on the sound mixer. The audio output from the sound mixer connects to the audio input of the VCR.

Mixers have more than one audio input, so other sound sources can also be plugged into them. You can mix the sound from your camcorder with inputs from other sound sources. Each of the inputs has a separate volume control, so you can fade them in and out to ensure a less important sound doesn't overshadow the main sound.

A good set up for sound mixing is to combine the original sound with a microphone for narration and a tape or CD player for music.

Background noise

For any occasion that has a high level of background noise, such as a street carnival or sporting event, the sound jumps every time you cut from one shot to another.

The way to shoot a colourful carnival is as a series of interesting shots.

To avoid the soundtrack jumping, you need to record a 'wildtrack'. A wildtrack is a continuous sound recording of an event. It should be recorded separately from the picture, using a tape recorder and omnidirectional microphone.

After the picture has been assemble edited into a final sequence, a portion of the wildtrack can be mixed with the original sound recorded by the camcorder. It provides a constant background that helps hide the visual cuts.

It is useful to build up a library of wildtracks on an audio tape. These could include five minutes of a football crowd, traffic, waves crashing and country sounds.

▶ These shots were taken at different times during the same event. Each time the camcorder is paused to compose another shot, the sound jumps. To prevent this, record a wildtrack of the general sound and mix it in with the picture and any other sound.

Adding music

With your camcorder and VCR connected together, you can start to build up more layers of sound. You can add commentary, music or sound effects to the existing sound, or replace it completely.

With an assembled sequence made up of images of the same subject, the sound may jump between shots, but it is as likely that the sound is uninteresting and needs replacing.

It may be best to scrap the original sound completely and record music over the entire sequence. Always pick an appropriate piece of music that reinforces the visual theme.

There are two ways you can do this, depending on the type of recorder you are using. If you have a VCR with audio dub, record the music directly on to the assembled sequence by plugging the music source into the video recorder and using the audio dub facility.

If yours doesn't have audio dub, you have to record the music on to the copy tape at the same time as you copy the picture.

If you need to assemble edit the sequence first, this means you must copy the assembled video on to a third tape, mixing in the music at the same time. This reduces the quality of the picture, although Hi8 and S-VHS suffer less loss from copying than VHS and 8mm.

Some music is labelled copyright-free, but remember to obtain the copyright holder's permission for other types of recording.

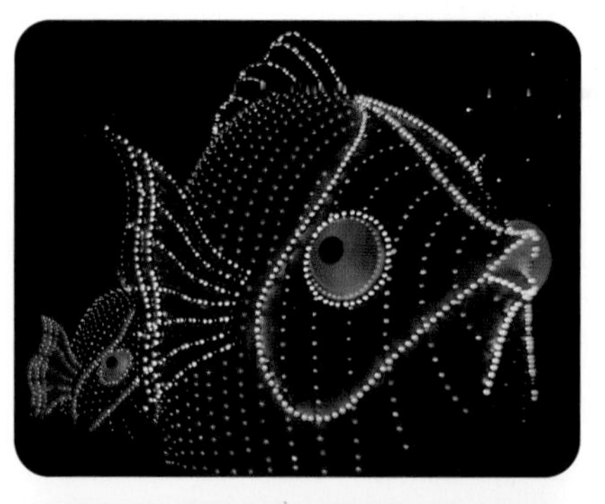

◀▼ This series of shots is let down by a rather tinny and muddled soundtrack. None of the original sound is necessary, so we can record over the entire sound track and start again. The best thing to do is cut out the original sound completely and record an appropriate piece of music over the top during editing.

Adding commentary

Commentary can be added to your video by plugging a microphone into the VCR and speaking at the appropriate moment. Add commentary to other sound, too, such as the existing recording or wildtrack.

If you are feeding all the sounds through a mixer, you can fade down the other sounds while you are speaking, and fade them up again when you have finished.

Prepare your commentary beforehand and practise reading out the script. If you are sitting close to the television set, turn the volume down. If the mic is too close to the TV's loudspeaker, a high-pitched noise, known as 'howl round', is recorded.

Thinking in sequences

Unless you direct the action in your video, you can't anticipate everything that happens. But you can ensure your video has structure by dividing it up into manageable portions, known as sequences.

Beware backspacing

When you start shooting, allow for backspace time. At the beginning of each shot, the camcorder rewinds slightly then reverses direction, moving forward to the end of the last edit. This is so the edit is clean.

Recorded tape contains control pulses and, by backspacing in this way, the camcorder matches the pulses between shots. This means the camcorder only starts recording about a second after you press the record button. So switch on a second or so before the action you want to capture begins.

◀▼ ***The cameraman has moved from a long shot to a mid shot. Both shots of the girl are fine by themselves, but when played back she appears to jump across the screen. Think of shots as a sequence. If you are always aware of the previous shot, you can avoid jump cuts.***

Videos are made up of shots. Shots can be of various types (for example static, zoom, pan, tilt) and different sizes (such as long shot, mid shot and close-up).

A series of shots of the same subject matter is a sequence. The task of planning and shooting a video is a lot easier if you think of it in terms of sequences instead of individual shots, and set about shooting one sequence at a time.

A new sequence begins when the action, location or time changes. When you record a shot, be aware of the shot that went before it and the shot that follows. You should already be careful to avoid crossing the line, but make sure, too, that the subject's position in the frame doesn't alter drastically from shot to shot.

If you move from a long shot of a person at the left hand side of the frame to a mid shot or close-up of a person towards the right of the frame, the person appears to jump – even though both shots may be perfectly composed.

Pace and rhythm

The order in which different types and sizes of shot follow each other, and the length of time each shot lasts, help determine the rhythm and pace of the action.

Pace refers to the average length of each shot and rhythm to the regularity of longer and shorter shots. A series of regular shots that last for several seconds suits a slow, restful subject. A variety of lengths suits fast and exciting action.

Fast pace and rhythm are most effective when they build up from a slow start. Start with a series of regular, lengthy shots and, as the pace of the action increases, step up the pace of the shots to match.

A good technique for recording really fast action is to mix a lot of short shots with the occasional lengthier shot that contains a lot of movement. The lengthier shots can also be pans – which help to re-establish the action.

First shots

◀ ***The classic way of opening a sequence is to use an establishing shot, which gives information about the location. This shot of Las Vegas could come before the action that takes place in a casino, club or restaurant.***

Once you start to think of your video as a collection of sequences assembled in a logical order, the next stage is to plan each one.

Like a good book, every sequence should have a start, a middle and an end. The opening shot should lead you into the subject, and the closing shot round off the action.

There may be a jump between sequences in both time and place, and you have to convey this at the start of each new one. The job of the opening shot is to establish the location. This is essential if you want the viewer to follow what is going on in your video.

Setting scenes

The conventional way to start a sequence is with a long shot. This generally contains more information than a mid shot or close-up, and can reveal more about a scene.

For instance, if your sequence involves people walking around a city, open with a shot of a recognizable landmark. If your sequence takes place in a hotel, open with a shot of the hotel, making sure you include the name.

As the shots in your sequence are likely to be of the same subject, it is tempting to record it all from the same position, moving only to follow the action.

In some instances, when you would miss something unrepeatable by pausing your camcorder, this is unavoidable. But if you have some control over the action, and can freely pause your camcorder to recompose, vary the angle and size of shots. This helps to make your video more interesting visually.

Closing shots

In most TV commercials, no matter how fast the pace has been throughout the ad, the final shot is always held for at least a second. This acts as a visual full stop.

Similarly, your sequence might contain a selection of zooms, pans and tilts, but the closing shot of the sequence should also be held for a second or two. This conveys to the viewer that the sequence has ended.

A shot showing somebody going through a door and closing it behind them could come at any point in a sequence. If the shot cuts immediately to another room, the implication is that the room is on the other side of the door.

If the camera stays on the closed door for a second or two, the viewer knows the sequence has ended. You have inserted your own full stop.

Another way of ending a scene is to have the action withdraw from the camera. The subject could be a person walking away, but a car driving into the distance or a boat sailing down a river would work as well.

The third classic method is to withdraw the camcorder from the action. Pan away from the main subject to something that is not important to the action, such as a painting or ornament, and hold it while the sound slowly fades away.

▲ ***Two classic ways of ending a sequence are to withdraw the camera from the subject or withdraw the subject from the camera. A good example is to hold a shot of someone walking away from the camera.***

Between sequences

Smooth cuts between shots are desirable, as they help your video to flow. They hide the fact that many minutes may have been compressed into, say, 20 seconds enabling you to cut out all the uneventful moments and concentrate on the interesting events.

When you move from one sequence to another, however, you want to tell the viewer the subject matter has changed. This can be done by starting your sequences with an establishing shot, but for variety there are more interesting ways of moving between sequences.

Fade away

One technique is to use the fade button fitted to most camcorders. This fades the sound down completely and the picture to either black or white. Don't overuse this feature – it is not appropriate for moving between every sequence.

Fades suggest to the viewer that time has elapsed. So don't use them to cut between two sequences that take place around the same time.

Another way of getting from one sequence to another is by using link shots. This involves starting a scene on a similar subject to the one on which you ended the last.

This could be a close-up of any object that features in both scenes – such as a glass or an ornament. It doesn't have to be an identical object. In the film *Lawrence of Arabia*, there is a classic link shot between the desert sun and a candle, with the flame in the same part of the frame as the sun.

◀ ***Fades are one of the most common ways of moving from one sequence to another, and are used to convey the passage of time. The subjects can be different.***

FADE DOWN

FADE UP

▶ ***In this sequence, the subject matter remains the same, but time has elapsed. A three or four second fade manages to show an hour or so passing.***

Tip

Plan ahead

For a simple video of, say, a family day out or a party, you won't be able to plan every shot in advance. But you can have a rough idea of what sequences you want to include. You have to be adaptable, as unforeseen events may happen, but you can at least plan ahead on the basis of what you know about your subject. For instance, if you are videoing a formal occasion, make sure you know when the speeches are taking place. Similarly, on a school athletics day, get a copy of the order of events beforehand. You can then roughly plan the sequences you want to shoot, and your video will end up a lot tighter than if you simply turn up and start recording.

PROJECT

On safari 2

A video of a day out to a safari park or zoo is a lot more interesting to watch if you structure it by splitting it up into sequences.

You can plan a lot of these in advance, as most safari parks have set events that occur at specific times, such as a seal show or feeding time.

The pace of the video should match the action. Use short shots to match the excitement of the animals at feeding time, and slow down the pace by using longer shots later in the afternoon, when most of the animals are grazing or resting.

With set pieces, such as a performing sea lion, you only need to capture a few minutes of the total display. To avoid the cuts jumping, shoot a trick and then insert a reaction shot from the crowd.

Later on cut back to another trick. This makes it look as if you have shot a continuous sequence, when in fact you've only recorded the highlights. In this way you can condense time to make a half hour display last only a few minutes.

▼ ***The two sea lion tricks in the left and right hand shots could have happened several minutes apart – with a lot of talking and waiting in between. Interesting as the tricks may be, the sequence might start to get a bit tedious if you record the whole show. What you need to do is record highlights and condense the show into a few minutes. If you record separate sequences and then add a shot of the crowd in between each time, you hide the fact that you have condensed time.***

▲ ***Another way of starting a sequence – particularly if the subject is static – is to pick out an interesting close-up, then slowly zoom out to reveal the whole subject. Here the sequence starts with the shoulder armour of a sleeping rhino.***

Between the shots

The aim when cutting between shots is to advance the action smoothly. Do it right and the viewer is gripped; do it wrong and confusion follows.

▲ *A mid shot is the most logical shot to cut to from a long short. It focuses the viewers' attention on the important subject, but isn't too dramatic a change in size.*

▲ *A full length shot of the couple starts the scene, but which shot should you cut to?*

▲ *An 'indecisive' cut occurs when you change the size of the subject in the frame by only a small amount between shots. The subject appears to jump.*

◀ *A 'shock' cut occurs when the subject size is changed dramatically. This should be used only when you want to jolt people. Otherwise, it has an unpleasantly jarring effect.*

Every video is made up of 'shots' – uninterrupted pieces of recording. Every time you press the record button you record another shot. When you pause or stop recording before you record a second shot, this is known as a 'cut'.

For instance, if you record a shot of a person, followed by a shot of a house, you have cut from a shot of a person to a shot of a house.

When you record two shots of the same subject, you have the opportunity to recompose the subject in the viewfinder. When you recompose, you can change either the size of the subject in the frame – say from a long shot to a mid shot – or the angle from which you shoot. Ideally, change the size *and* angle between shots.

If you watch a movie or television, you may not be aware of the cuts between shots – even though there are probably several a minute. This is because, in most instances, the aim is to make the cuts invisible.

If you change neither subject size nor the angle you shoot from, the subject appears to jump in the frame. This fault is known as a 'jump' cut – avoid it, unless you want to shock the viewer.

Changing shot size

When you change the size of the subject in the frame between shots, you should make the change significant enough to be noticeable, but not so great that it jolts the viewer.

For instance, if your first shot is a long shot of two people walking arm in arm, the ideal cut is to a mid shot of the two people cut off just above the waist.

Indecisive cuts

If you change the size of the subject in the frame by only a small amount, this has the same effect as not changing the size at all.

For instance, if you were to cut from the long shot of the couple walking arm in arm to a shot that cuts them off just below the knees, the subject still appears to jump between shots. This type of cut is known as an 'indecisive' cut.

Shock cuts

The opposite of an indecisive cut is a 'shock' cut. This is when the size of the shot in the frame changes so much from long shot to close-up that it jolts the viewer.

A shock cut from the couple walking might be to a close-up of one of their faces. Avoid this unless your aim is to shock the viewer – by cutting to a close-up of the girl screaming, for instance – when a shock cut would be appropriate.

Angling for change

When cutting between shots, you can change the angle you shoot the subject from, as well as the size of the subject in the frame.

You have to be careful with moving subjects, however. If you cut between a shot taken from one side of the subject and one taken from the other side, the subject appears to change directions between shots.

It is easy to avoid this disconcerting change of direction if you imagine that the moving subject paints a line on the ground as it moves, ahead as well as behind. So long as you keep shooting from the same side of this line, the subject appears to move in the same direction, and you won't confuse the viewer.

Don't cross that line!

This is one of the most basic rules in video, and is sometimes called the 180° rule. Another way of stating it is to say: don't cross that line!

However, a way of crossing the line correctly is to take a neutral shot along the line itself, with your subject moving towards you, and insert it between the two other shots.

From a neutral shot you can move to either side without confusing the viewer. For instance, shoot the first shot of the person moving to the right, the second moving towards the camcorder and the third moving to the left. This way, you have correctly crossed the line without confusing the viewer.

◀ ***From position A, the man is walking left to right across the screen. As he continues on his journey and you change camera position for the next shot, he should continue to move from left to right.***

▶ ***From position B, the man appears to be moving from right to left. If this shot follows a shot from position A, the man will appear to have reversed direction.***

▼ ***A man walks along a path towards a door. You can change the angle you shoot from between shots, but you must be careful not to cross the line.***

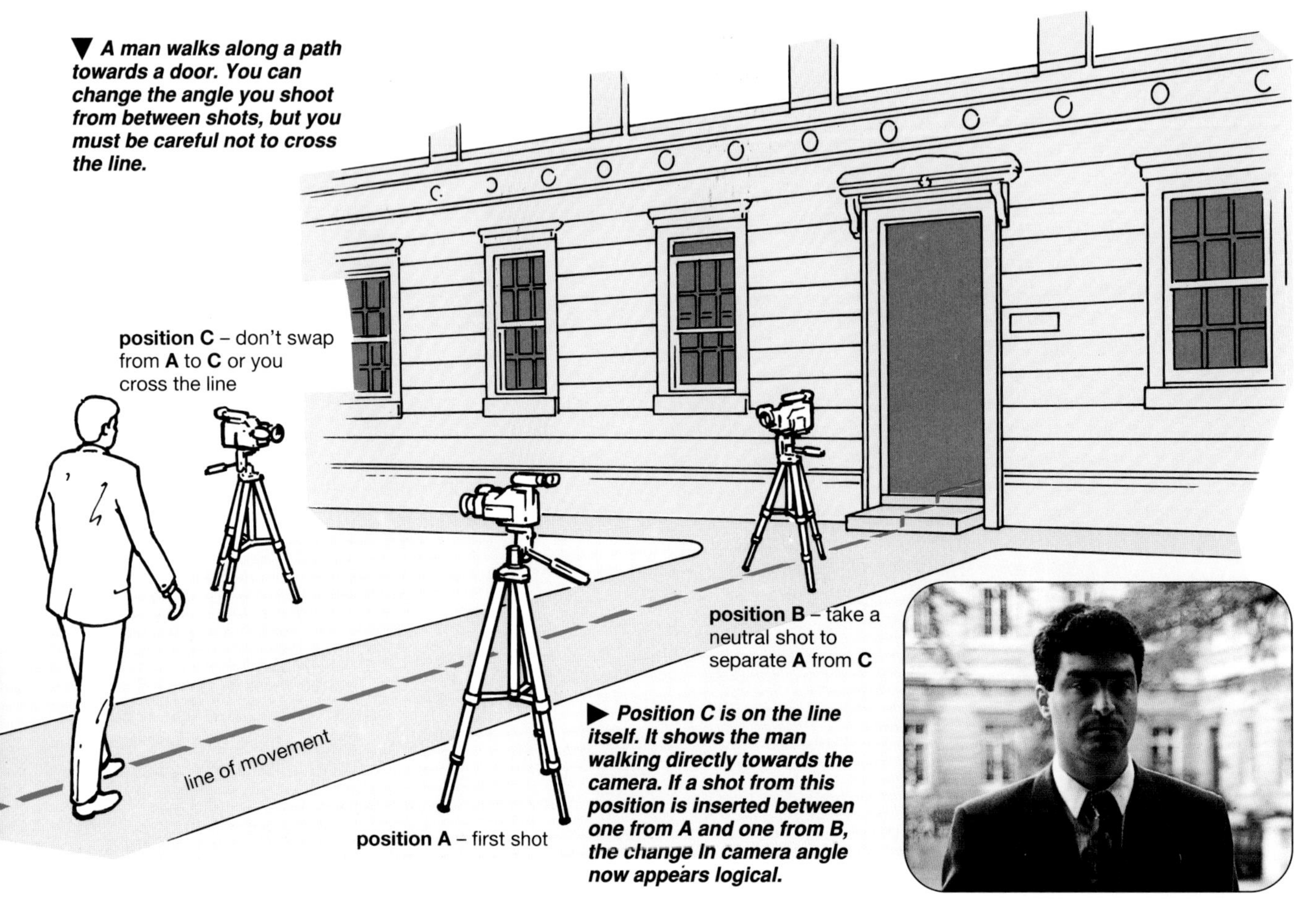

▶ ***Position C is on the line itself. It shows the man walking directly towards the camera. If a shot from this position is inserted between one from A and one from B, the change in camera angle now appears logical.***

Through the door

When you video somebody walking through a door, you have to move with the camcorder from one side of the door to the other. Your first shot might be of the back of the person going through the door and your second of them entering the room on the other side.

The important thing to remember is that the subject is moving and still 'painting' an imaginary line. The line continues into the room on the other side of the door. If you shoot the person entering the room from their right side, you should shoot the second shot from their right side too. Otherwise, they will again appear to have changed direction.

Again, you can shoot from on the line itself.

▶ ***As the man reaches the doorway, he moves past camera position D. You should shoot the next shot from inside. As the line continues through the doorway, make sure you don't cross it.***

▲ ***From position D you can pan round to follow the man as he passes the camera position and makes his way up the steps. In this shot, he is still travelling from left to right.***

▲ ***Position E is inside the hallway and on the same side of the line as position D. This is the logical position to take the next shot from.***

▲ ***Position F is on the other side of the line to position D. The man now moves from right to left. He appears to have changed direction.***

PROJECT Crossing the line

The problems with crossing the line are far easier to understand when you see the effects for yourself. Take a simple scene, such as somebody being let in through a front door.

Shoot the scene twice, both times using four very simple shots taken from the positions below. The first example obeys the 180° rule about not crossing the line, the second ignores it. As soon as you play your video back, you will notice why the rule is so important.

In the first example, the person knocking on the door is always moving from left to right across the scene, and the person answering the door is moving from right to left. In the second example, there is no logical movement.

CHECK IT!

When filming people remember that:

- ❏ Moving subjects generate an imaginary line along the path of their movement.
- ❏ If you cross this line with the camera between shots the subject appears to have reversed direction.
- ❏ A neutral shot along the line – from in front of or behind the subject – can follow or come before a shot from either side of the line. If inserted between shots taken from different sides of the line, neutral shots provide a correct way of crossing from one side to the other.

Shot 1: taken from position A. The subject moves along the path from left to right. Pan round to follow her as she walks towards the door.

Shot 2: taken from position B. Close-up of the girl as she knocks on the door. Note how she is still moving from left to right.

Shot 3: from position C. Static shot positioned back from the door. The second person moves into the frame from the right and answers the door. You see the caller framed in the doorway.

Shot 4: back to position B as the caller walks through the door and it is closed after her. If you go on to shoot a further sequence in the house, the next shot should again not be from the other side of the line.

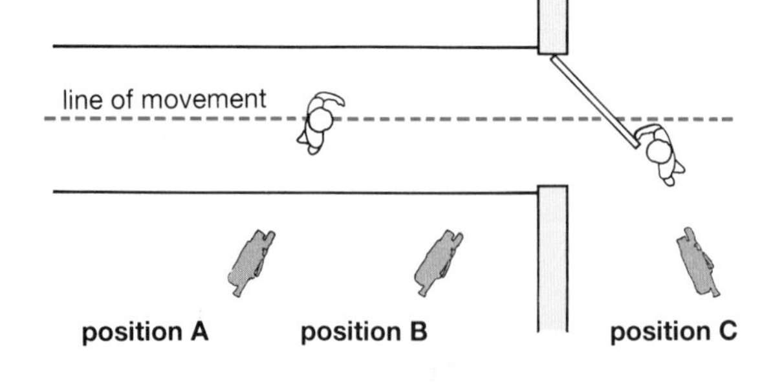

Shot 1: from position A. Same as in the first sequence. Shot panning past caller as she moves up the path. Subject moving from left to right.

Shot 2: from position D, which this time is on the other side of the line. Although it might seem a reasonable position from which to shoot the person knocking, when played back you notice she is moving from left to right – in the opposite direction from the last shot.

Shot 3: from position C. Another problem here. Both subjects appear to be moving from left to right – even though, logically, the two are moving in the opposite direction.

Shot 4: back to position D. This whole sequence when played back looks utterly confusing because of the constant line-crossing.

position D

line of movement

position A

position C

The power of suggestion

When you cut from one subject to another, the viewer automatically sees a link between the two subjects. This allows you to suggest relationships that don't really exist, and is a powerful method of advancing your story.

Viewers of your home video should only be aware of the finished result, not the techniques employed. When you pause after a shot, it may be some time before you record the next. However, on screen the two shots appear to take place straight after each other.

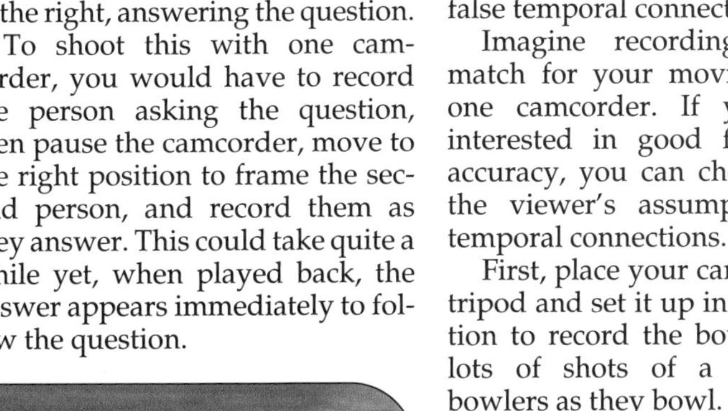

Imagine a two shot sequence. The first shot shows a person looking to the left, asking a question. The second shows a person looking to the right, answering the question.

To shoot this with one camcorder, you would have to record the person asking the question, then pause the camcorder, move to the right position to frame the second person, and record them as they answer. This could take quite a while yet, when played back, the answer appears immediately to follow the question.

Time link

People watching have made what is known as a 'temporal connection' – they assume one action follows on immediately from another. As long as you record two shots that appear to show continuous action, you can create completely false temporal connections.

Imagine recording a cricket match for your movie with only one camcorder. If you're more interested in good footage than accuracy, you can cheat by using the viewer's assumptions about temporal connections.

First, place your camcorder on a tripod and set it up in a good position to record the bowler. Record lots of shots of a selection of bowlers as they bowl.

Next, move your camcorder to a good position to record the batsman (remembering not to cross the line of action, which cuts the pitch in half along the line of the wicket). Record several shots of a number of batsmen in action, starting the shot while the bowler is running.

To add a bit more interest to your video, you can shoot some close-ups of faces and a few wide shots of the whole wicket to show the batsmen running or the ball being hit to the boundary.

When you edit, record a shot of one of the bowlers and follow it by a good shot of the batsman hitting the ball. But don't include the same person in both shots. The connection is so strong that the viewer assumes it is the same delivery.

▲ ***The shot of the bowler comes from your stock of bowler shots, recorded from the same position. You don't need to pan the camera to follow the ball, because you are going to cut to a shot of the batsman.***

▶ ***This shot was recorded at the same match, but possibly half an hour after the shot of the bowler. When edited together, the temporal connection is so strong the viewer assumes they occur in the same time scale as they appear on the screen.***

Leaps of logic

The viewer's willingness to believe the story you show on the video can be used to imply connections between subjects when there is no connection. This form of cheating is used all the time in the movies.

Imagine, for instance, you are shooting a video of a foreign holiday. To link the shots in your own country with those in your destination, you might want a shot of your aeroplane landing.

Such a shot is impossible if you are on the plane yourself. The obvious solution is to shoot another plane landing at the airport. The viewer will not question the fact that it is your plane.

Another common cheat is to use an incorrect establishing shot. If you want to shoot a scene in a video that is supposed to take place inside a particular building, you might find it difficult to get permission to shoot there.

The answer again is to record a shot of the outside of a building and follow it by a shot of people inside. The viewer assumes the second shot takes place inside the building featured in the first shot. This is known as a 'logical connection'.

◀▼ ***Jump cuts – where we only vary our position slightly when cutting to another shot of the same subject – draw attention to the edit. Normally, this is undesirable, but here it ensures the viewer notices the subject. From these three shots, each showing a closer view of the building, we cut to a shot of businessmen in an office. The viewer automatically assumes they are within the building.***

Tip: Spatial awareness

A third suggestive cut in video is the 'spatial connection'. This is where one shot indicates where the next shot takes place.

For instance, we see a man at a desk. There is a knock at a door and he looks to the right. We cut to a person opening a door.

We haven't seen the door in relation to the man, but we assume it is off to his right.

A movie might cut between shots of people pointing and screaming and library shots of a lion. The lion never appears on screen at the same time as the people.

A kind of montage

Party mix

Montage sequences can be excellent ways of condensing a lot of activity into a very short space of time.

At a party, for instance, you may have a couple of dozen short shots of different guests enjoying themselves. From these, you can create a montage sequence lasting perhaps a minute and a half. Add music over the whole sequence.

Normally when we cut between shots we are telling a story. Each shot tells the viewer 'what happens next' in the narrative.

There is another common use of cutting between subjects, however, which is called montage. A montage is a collection of shots which are used to conjure up a feeling or idea.

Montage sequences fit into two main categories. The first is when we take a series of shots of the same subject to build up a picture of that subject.

Character building

For instance, if we are shooting a montage of a person, we could show a number of shots, including an expensive watch on their wrist, a close-up of their face and an old school tie. These close-up details can tell us a lot about a subject in a small space of time by concentrating the viewer's attention on relevant information.

Another sequence might show us three or four shots of houses with For Sale notices – some of which are weather-beaten and have obviously been there for some time. In a few seconds, we build up a picture of recession.

The second kind of montage is when we show a number of different subjects to build up a whole picture. For instance, a classic way of expressing the concept of spring is to show a shot of a lamb, followed by a shot a flower opening, followed by a shot of children playing.

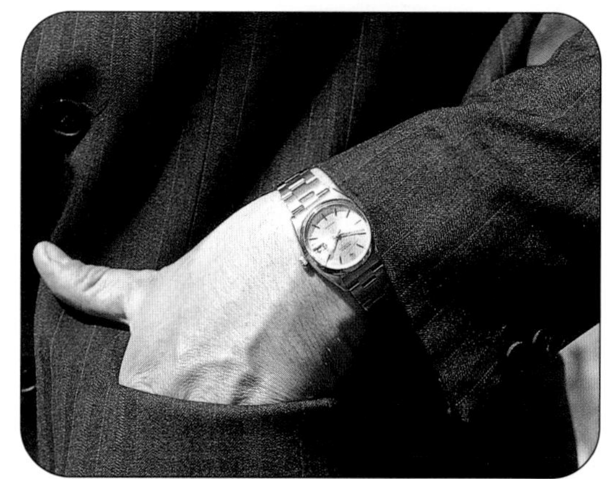

◄▼ ***In this montage sequence, the first three shots – of a well-groomed man, his old school tie and his expensive watch – paint a picture of a powerful businessman or a local dignitary. In the fourth shot, however, the scuffed heels suggest another dimension to this person and, therefore, a story worth pursuing.***

PROJECT Getting suggestive

Try out the power of suggestion yourself by recording three shots that work on the viewers' desire to make sense of what they are seeing. You need a couple of friends to help you out.

Each shot should last only a few seconds. You can use this technique over and over again. If executed correctly, it won't be noticed.

▶ ***Record a few seconds of a static shot of a house or building. Viewers seeing this house immediately assume that this is where the action takes place. It would be best to find an interesting location that doesn't have obstacles, such as rows of parked cars, in front of it.***

▶ ***Find a different location and record a shot of someone sitting in a chair reading a book. To anybody watching, this person is inside the house shown in the first shot. Next, get someone to knock on a door out of shot. The seated subject should then move their head to the right and say "come in" – even if they are in reality staring at a wall.***

▶ ***Move to a completely different room – or preferably a different house. Record a shot from the point of view of the seated subject in the second shot of someone else opening a door and saying "hello". The camcorder should be positioned low down, so that it is about the same distance from the ground as the seated subject's eyes.***

Crop in fairly close on the person at the door, in case the completely different decor gives the shot away. If you really want to confuse the viewer, use the same person in both shots. So strong is the power of suggestion that they may assume it is an identical twin at the door!

The gadget bag

Although everything you need for a video shoot is included in your camcorder, video accessories can make shooting more convenient and your results more professional.

▼ ***A gadget bag is a useful item to have with you at the seaside. It won't prevent your equipment from being ruined if a wave soaks it – but it will protect it from salt spray.***

With equipment getting smaller and smaller you can now take your camcorder anywhere you'd take your stills camera. Wherever you go, whether it's a day trip to the seaside or a fortnight's holiday abroad, taking your camcorder can provide you with an unrepeatable visual record of your trip.

Choosing accessories

Once you've packed your camcorder neatly into its travelling case, you have to decide if there is any other equipment you need to take with you.

There are as many types of accessory in video as there are in photography and, though you won't need all of them all of the time, each comes into its own in different circumstances.

If you are new to video, it is unlikely that you have all the accessories listed in this chapter. The next three pages should help you decide how useful each is to you, so you can choose which you want to suit your shooting needs.

Travelling light

When you venture far afield, you should be prepared – but you shouldn't weigh yourself down. In many instances, the best idea is to travel light. What you take should depend on your method of transport and where you're staying.

If you're going by car and are staying where there's plenty of room, you can take as much equipment as you like. If your trip involves flying or lots of walking, you should only take as much as is practical.

Think realistically about the shooting opportunities you are likely to have. Be selective about what you take if most of your trip involves activities where using your camcorder is impractical.

There are some accessories you can always take with you because they're so small. Polarizing filters, for instance, eliminate the reflections you get when shooting through glass or when there is water in the scene. They also deepen blue skies and whiten clouds. Yet they can fit into tiny side pockets on your camcorder bag.

▲ ***Polarizing filters deepen blues and make whites more brilliant. They also eliminate reflections, found on sunlit waters and snow.***

Tip: Travellers' checks

Apart from the bore of having to carry lots of heavy equipment, there are other things to consider when travelling abroad.

- ❑ Make sure all your equipment is insured.
- ❑ Always carry your camcorder as hand luggage when flying, because normal baggage tends to get thrown around a lot.
- ❑ Take receipts for everything, to prove that you didn't buy the equipment abroad, or ask outgoing customs to compile a list.
- ❑ X-ray machines won't damage tapes, but searching devices that generate strong electromagnetic fields might. The safest option is to ask for all your equipment to be hand-searched. Allow extra time at check-in.
- ❑ If your battery charger is the old type that is not switchable and the voltage is different in the country you are going to, take a voltage transformer.

In the bag

Some accessories, like a spare battery, are vital, while others, such as extra lights, you may only use sometimes or when you become more advanced. Use this guide to pick and choose.

Microphones

In any situation where the sound you want to record risks being overwhelmed by general noise, a microphone placed near the subject can help overcome this problem.

There are various types of microphone available, from omnidirectional, which record equally in all directions, to unidirectional, which only pick up sounds from one direction. Unidirectional microphones have a greater range than the microphones built into camcorders. Stick to microphones in the 200-600 ohms range.

VERDICT: For everyday work, your camcorder's built-in microphone is fine, but as you get more advanced you will find an add-on mic more useful.

Filters

There are many special effect and creative filters available, but a handful of more everyday filters are all you need in ordinary shooting situations.

Perhaps the most useful is a skylight filter, which cuts out distant haze. Apart from this, it has very little effect, but you can keep it on the lens to protect it whenever you're shooting.

Polarizing filters are also useful in any scene where there is a lot of reflection.

VERDICT: Filters are dealt with on pages 55-56, but a skylight filter is worth buying, as it provides another line of defence against damage to the lens.

Lights

Although camcorders can shoot in candlelight, the colours tend to be dull and the image flat. To brighten up your subject, a simple video light attached to the top of your camcorder can do the trick.

The ideal shooting conditions are outside in bright sunlight, when you don't need a light.

VERDICT: You probably won't need a light for daytime shooting, but if you shoot people indoors or outside in the dark, you get much better results using one.

Battery

A battery charger comes with your camcorder, but you can buy portable units that can be powered by the car battery. Carry one with you whenever you venture out of your house.

Probably the most useful accessory you can buy is a spare battery. This enables you to have one on charge constantly.

VERDICT: One extra battery is essential. If you're doing a lot of shooting away from home, a couple of spares or a battery belt might come in handy.

Converters

Lens converters modify the focal length of the lens. This means if you don't think your 6X, 8X or 12X zoom is great enough, you can make your lens even longer by adding a teleconverter or wider by adding a wide angle converter.

Teleconverters enable you to video subjects that are even smaller or further away than you'd be able to see with the telephoto end of the zoom lens. But note that, with long telephotos, depth of field becomes very narrow.

Wide angle converters allow you to see more of a scene than you would with the wide angle end of the zoom. This gives you more versatility in enclosed spaces, but close vertical lines at the edge of the frame can appear to bend.

Reversible wide/tele converters that combine both functions are available.

VERDICT: The telephoto end of a camcorder is already fairly long – normally the equivalent of about 300mm on a 35mm camera. Wide angle converters are more useful, particularly when shooting in small rooms indoors.

Bags

If you have only a few accessories, you can carry them in the same bag as your camcorder. A soft bag is the handiest because it weighs least. Once you have built up a collection of accessories, though, you may want to invest in a separate bag for them.

Many video bags have removable dividers, so you can arrange the bag to fit your own equipment.
VERDICT: Initially, you need a bag to carry your camcorder and a few accessories in. Buy a bigger bag when you have more to put in it.

Supports

The better camcorder tripods have pan and tilt heads as here, so the picture changes smoothly as you turn the camcorder up and down or from side to side. Mini tripods and chest supports are also available – they're not as sturdy but more suited to holiday packing.

If you only want something to help support your camcorder, a monopod is generally cheaper and more compact, and some even double as microphone booms for when you're using an add-on mic.

Don't use a tripod designed for a stills camera. It won't be all that much use for your camcorder. Most cheap camera tripods are not strong enough to support the larger camcorders properly.
VERDICT: The difference between a wobbly video and one where the camcorder is still is enormous. If you intend to use pan or tilt shots, or hold static shots for any length of time, some kind of support is a must. A tripod is particularly useful when using the telephoto end of the camera's zoom range, as camera shake is more noticeable at tele settings.

Lens cloths

There are many ways of cleaning your lens, but be careful not to use anything abrasive that might scratch it. Special lens cleaning cloths are available now that don't scratch, but can be machine washed. Don't use tissues, as they can scratch.
VERDICT: A special lens cleaning cloth is best, or a spectacle cleaning cloth if it is not silicone impregnated.

Tape

Tape length varies from format to format. If you're using a full-sized VHS tape you can get up to four or five hours' shooting in standard play mode. 8mm tapes generally give twice the running time of VHS-C.
VERDICT: It's advisable to carry at least one spare. Blank tapes are the same all over the world, so unless you're going completely into the wild, you don't need to take loads with you.

Headphones

Not all camcorders have headphone sockets. If yours does, a set of headphones – even a cheap pair – enables you to monitor the sound as the camcorder records it, as well as letting you listen to the sound recording on play back.
VERDICT: If your camcorder has a headphone socket, investing in headphones, or even earphones, is inexpensive and worthwhile.

Power play

For your camcorder to work, you have to power it. Camcorders can run off the mains, via a car adapter or directly from a NiCad (Nickel Cadmium) battery.

NiCad batteries are the most commonly used power supply because they are so convenient. You get one battery with your camcorder, but a second is a sound investment, so you always have one recharged and ready to use when the other runs out.

An alternative available for some batteries is an EBP (extra battery pack), particularly useful if you're away from home for some time. An EBP is a hollow shell the same size as a battery which takes normal batteries.

This means that, so long as there is a shop selling batteries, you're never out of supply. They're expensive to keep replacing, but dry cells normally have a 50% longer life than NiCads.

If you stick with NiCads, remember that they can be temperamental, so treat them with care. Here are a few tips on how to get the most out of your battery:

❑ **Recharging** It takes about an hour to recharge a battery from flat. Ensure the battery is fully charged before you start shooting, because it helps you gauge how much recording time you have.

❑ **How much power?** You can get an hour's shooting from some of the more powerful batteries, but remember that electronic functions, such as zooming and reviewing what you've shot, guzzle battery power. If you zoom to reframe the shot while the camcorder is in pause mode, use the manual zoom. Only review if it is essential.

❑ **The chemicals** inside the NiCad battery are very sensitive to temperature. When charging, do so at room temperature. Charging in a cold environment takes longer, while if it is too hot you run the risk of the battery not fully charging.

❑ **Flat battery** Make sure the battery is fully discharged (flat) before you recharge it. If you keep recharging the battery when it is already half charged you run the risk of permanently lowering the maximum power of the battery.

❑ **Removing the battery** NiCads discharge slowly when connected to the camcorder. If you pause in your shooting schedule for an hour or two, remove the battery.

❑ **Storing** Be careful how you store your battery. It's best to store NiCads flat in cool environments. Fully discharge your battery before you store it, as this helps maintain its life.

❑ **Short circuit** Make sure the contact terminals on a charged battery don't get connected to each other by a conductive material, such as metal – don't put a battery in your pocket with your keys. This leads to a short circuit, which overheats the battery, making it useless.

▲ ***If your camera has manual zoom, use it to recompose shots when in pause mode, to preserve battery power.***

▲ ***Don't leave the battery on the camcorder when not in use. Take it off and store it separately.***

◀ ***When storing your battery, put it down flat in a cool place.***

Using filters

As an advanced video user, you can enhance or alter a shot with filters – but you may need to override some of your camcorder's automatic features.

Once you master the basics of video, it is worth exploring how you can improve or even introduce special effects into your shots with filters. Just as in stills photography, filters screw on to the front of the camcorder's lens.

A number of photographic filters, such as skylight and ultra-violet, have little image alteration use in video. However, it is worth attaching one semi-permanently to protect the front element of the lens. Some companies market dedicated protection filters.

Polarizing filters are as useful in video as in stills photography. They darken blue skies, but as they have no colour of their own, do not add a cast to the rest of the scene. If your shot has a mixture of clouds and blue sky, the sky is deepened by a polarizer, but the clouds remain white. Polarizing filters also eliminate reflections on glass or water.

◀ As in stills photography, a polarizing filter can improve the look of a shot. It deepens blue skies without altering the colour of the rest of the image, but also eliminates unwanted reflections from glass and water.

The other standard filter is the neutral density (ND) filter. It reduces the amount of light entering the lens. This is useful in exceedingly bright conditions, such as on a sunny beach. The only other way of reducing the amount of light is to use a fast shutter speed, which could cause strobing.

The other use of the ND filter is to narrow the depth of field to pick out a subject from its surroundings. By cutting down the light, you force the camcorder to open the iris to compensate, reducing in turn the depth of field.

▲ Use a dedicated protection filter to protect your lens. Filters come in various sizes, so check in your camcorder's instruction manual to see what size it takes.

Special effects

The simplest special effects filters are the diffusers and softeners. Softeners are mild diffusers which reduce the sharpness of the image slightly.

Strong diffusers soften the image a great deal, causing an effect that is often used in the movies to show dream sequences. Mild softeners can be used to add a fairy-tale quality to wedding ceremonies or baby pictures.

Even more extreme are fog filters, which reduce the contrast in an image so that, although distant objects are still visible, the scene looks as if it is shrouded in thin mist.

Special effects filters have limited use in video, but often find a place in title sequences. Spot filters, for instance, diffuse the edges of the image, so that the sharp image is contained in a circle in the centre of the frame. An important subject can be placed within the vignette and the title overlaid.

These are often used to create a frame within a frame, to show the viewpoint of someone looking through a keyhole or binoculars.

There are several varieties of starburst filter. When these are used, points of bright light appear as starbursts. Others turn beams of light into streaks of colour.

◀ Starburst filters can give very dramatic results, as here, so they should be used selectively. A subject such as this may well look best as part of a title sequence.

▶ A soft focus filter takes away any harsh lighting, producing a pleasant, dreamy image. Use one when you're filming babies or for close-ups of people when you want them to look more attractive.

Colour correction

Not all light sources have the same colour temperature (see **Using available light**, opposite). Domestic bulbs are yellow, while overcast days produce very blue light.

To cope with these extremes in colour, camcorders can boost either the red, green or blue part of the video signal to achieve the correct colour balance.

The white balance sensor in most camcorders looks at the brightest part of the image and considers this to be white. If the brightest part is yellow, it reduces the amount of yellow in the scene to give a more natural colour.

In some situations, you may want to override the camcorder's colour balance system for dramatic effect. For instance, a red sunset makes an excellent closing shot for a scene, but it would be washed out if left to the camcorder, which would judge it to be indoor.

Check in your camcorder's manual to see if it senses white balance through the lens or via an external sensor. If it uses an external sensor, leave it on auto and add the appropriate filter to obtain the colour cast you want. If your camcorder measures light through the lens, fix the white balance by switching it to one of its presets.

▲ ***If you shoot a red sunset using the camcorder on auto white balance setting, the camcorder may detect the warm colour temperature and mistake it for an indoor scene. This boosts the blues and destroys the warmth. To compensate, use a red filter.***

Day for night

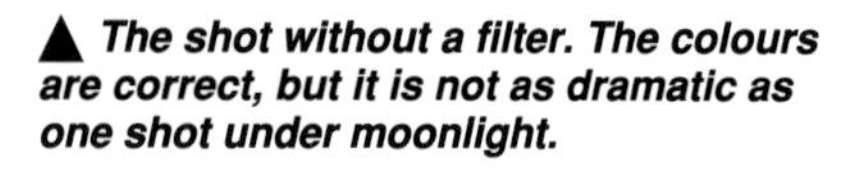

▲ ***The shot without a filter. The colours are correct, but it is not as dramatic as one shot under moonlight.***

▲ ***This was taken at the same time of day, but a blue filter and underexposure simulate moonlight.***

Blue filters can be used for a special form of video shooting known as 'day for night'. This is when you shoot during the day, while trying to make the video look as if it was shot under moonlight.

Day for night can look very atmospheric. But, as there is more light during the day, it's easier to obtain a clear image than when shooting at night under genuine moonlight.

A blue filter will add a blue cast to the picture, but to make the shot look more realistic, you should reduce the exposure slightly. If your camcorder doesn't allow independent control of the iris, you may be able to reduce the exposure by using a fast shutter.

However, be careful when shooting moving subjects, as they are prone to "strobing", or a rather jerky old-time-movie effect.

Using available light

In some lighting conditions, your camcorder might struggle to give the best results. But you can get round these problems – without buying extra lights.

The human eye adjusts to different lighting conditions automatically. Most camcorders now do the same, but there are older models that must be controlled manually, as well as advanced camcorders equipped with manual overrides.

Colours vary under different lighting conditions. This is most obvious with white objects, which look orange under a 60W light bulb, but under a bright sunlit sky have a bluish tint.

Keep whites right

In stills photography, there are two types of film for the two main lighting conditions. Normal 'daylight' film is balanced for the blue light of outdoor and flash photography and tungsten film is for use under artificial light.

The equivalent in video is white balance. White balance attempts to reproduce white objects as pure white – whatever colour they reflect from the surrounding light. Most systems do this automatically, boosting blue in indoor conditions and yellow outdoors.

Some camcorders have manual settings for indoor and outdoor shooting. Switch it to the correct position every time you move between indoors and out.

Others let you set white balance manually. Point the camcorder at a piece of white card and press the manual white balance button. The camcorder reproduces the card as white, reducing the amount of blue if the card has a bluish tint.

▼▶ Most camcorders compensate for colour casts on white objects. On systems you adjust manually, set white balance to the outdoor position, when outdoors. If you set to indoor, whites take on a bluish tint.

◀▲ When indoors, set white balance to the indoor position. As tungsten lights are yellow, the scene should still have a warm, yellowish glow. If you mistakenly leave the white balance on outdoor, the colours become far too yellow.

Contrast killing

The best condition to shoot in is bright daylight with light cloud or haze. Both disperse light and help lower contrast and harsh shadows.

Video sensors have less tolerance to high contrast than film. In stills photography, high contrast between highlight and shadow can look good. In video, it spells trouble.

If you use a camcorder to shoot a high contrast scene, with a light subject and dark background, the white highlights tend to burn out into bright unattractive areas.

If the scene you intend shooting includes strong areas of white and dark, change your position until you find a viewpoint with less contrast.

One way of doing this is to move to a position where the light source is to the side, rather than in front or behind you.

Another way is to zoom in so the subject is a lot closer, cutting out much of the dark background and so reducing contrast.

▲ This sunset could fool some white balance systems. Use a red or orange filter to compensate.

Drama scene

Certain weather conditions are not normally desirable because the colours are hard to capture successfully, but you might seek them out for specific reasons. For instance, orange sunsets make very atmospheric shots, but often have high contrast, which can disturb some white balance systems.

Because sunsets are often orange, rather than blue, your camcorder might assume it is indoors and try to compensate by boosting the blue light. This kills the effect of the dramatic deep orange light.

If you can set your camcorder's white balance manually, make sure it is set to daylight, so that it faithfully reproduces the reds and oranges. If not use an orange filter.

Lux level

The amount of light in a scene is known in video as the lux level. The brighter the surrounding light, the higher the lux level. All camcorders boast incredibly low minimum lux levels, so they can record images in very low light.

Lux aren't everything

Minimum lux levels vary between one and ten lux. Most indoor scenes are below 100 lux, but camcorders can normally handle this level. However, the lower the light level, the greater the risk of grey and grainy images.

The best lighting for video is outside in fairly bright sunlight. Colours look richer than under artificial light.

As you get more advanced, you may want to use additional video lights to boost the colour and detail in your image. But even without add-on lights you can improve the lighting inside by using stronger bulbs (but don't exceed the lampholder's capacity), bringing extra household lights or candles into the room and taking the shades off any lamps out of shot.

Don't point your camcorder directly at a bright source of light, such as a bulb or the sun, as this may damage the camcorder. In any case, if your subject is close, and the main source of light is behind it, it may throw the subject into shadow.

▶ 10,000 lux: outdoors on a sunlit day gives ideal shooting conditions. Colours are bright and no artificial lighting is required.

▶ 100 lux: indoors in daylight. This can be an awkward time to shoot, as contrast is low and colours subdued. You may have to rely on the daylight coming into the room to light your shot, but shoot across the light, rather than into it, as this gives the most even illumination.

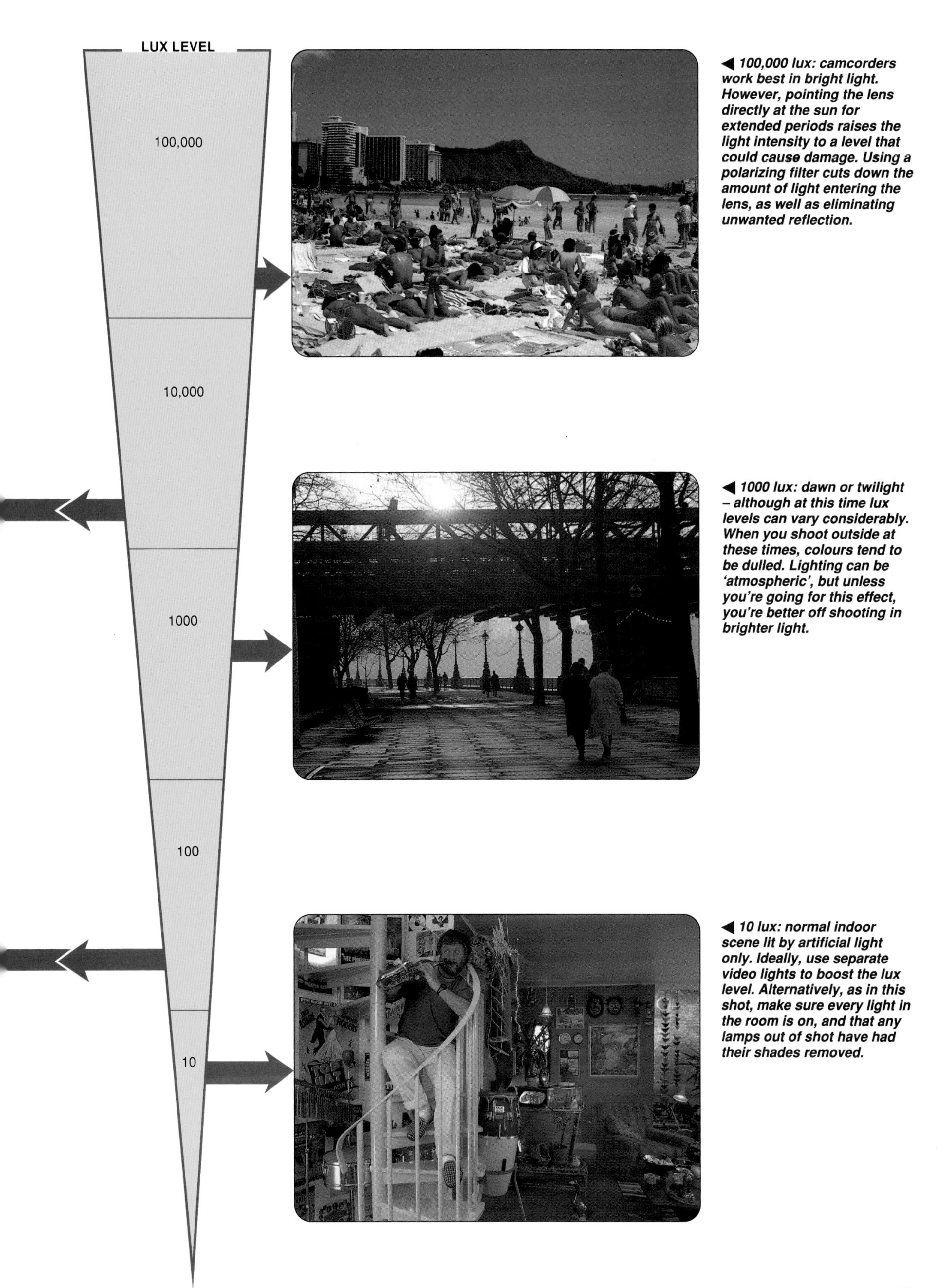

◀ ***100,000 lux: camcorders work best in bright light. However, pointing the lens directly at the sun for extended periods raises the light intensity to a level that could cause damage. Using a polarizing filter cuts down the amount of light entering the lens, as well as eliminating unwanted reflection.***

◀ ***1000 lux: dawn or twilight – although at this time lux levels can vary considerably. When you shoot outside at these times, colours tend to be dulled. Lighting can be 'atmospheric', but unless you're going for this effect, you're better off shooting in brighter light.***

◀ ***10 lux: normal indoor scene lit by artificial light only. Ideally, use separate video lights to boost the lux level. Alternatively, as in this shot, make sure every light in the room is on, and that any lamps out of shot have had their shades removed.***

Backlight complication

Although you want as much light as possible when shooting indoors, if you shoot a subject against a much brighter background, such as window light, you risk the subject being silhouetted.

In this situation, you can use the BLC (backlight compensation) button. Pressing this increases the amount of light passing through the lens, brightening the subject. However, if the contrast between the subject and the background is very great, pressing the BLC could cause the background to become too bright. This can cause white 'burn out' on the TV screen.

Mixed blessings

An alternative is to reflect some of the light back on to the subject. Specially designed reflectors are available, but crumpled silver paper, or even a large mirror, do equally well.

Another way of brightening up the subject is to use an artificial lamp pointing at the subject. However, although this lowers the contrast, it also gives rise to a mixture of bluish daylight and yellow/orange artificial light. The camcorder's white balance system cannot cope with mixed lighting.

In this case, you need to change the colour of one of the lights so that it matches the other. The easiest way to do this is to place a blue gel or filter over the artificial light, so that it matches the daylight.

◀ SUBJECT SILHOUETTED
Most rooms are dimly lit compared to outside, but you can raise illumination by placing your subject next to a window. However, the subject can be silhouetted by backlight.

▶ TOO MUCH BACKLIGHT
Pressing the BLC button increases the amount of light entering the lens, brightening up the subject. But this can cause the light coming through the window to look too bright.

▼ MAGIC MIRROR
With high contrast, a better alternative is to use a reflector – such as a mirror or kitchen foil – shining the window light back into the subject's face.

▶ MIXED LIGHT
Using an artificial light boosts the light level, but can cause odd-looking mixed lighting problems, where one side of the subject has a yellow tint, and the other a blue-white tint.

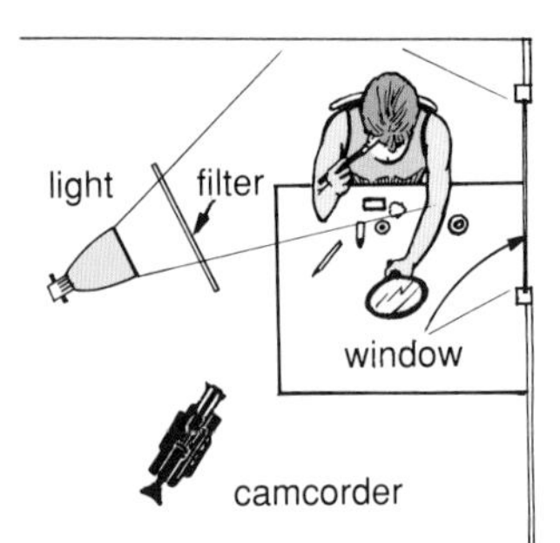

◀▶ FILTERING OUT
One way of coping with mixed lighting is to use a blue filter over the artificial light to match it with the daylight. This offers the most evenly lit and natural-looking solution. Set the camcorder's white balance to daylight setting.

Using add-on lights

Although most camcorders can cope with very low light, for better results it may be worth adding a little light of your own.

When used in low light, camcorders boost the 'gain' – the current supplied to the imaging chip. This increases the chip's sensitivity to light. Although this means the camcorder can record an image in low light, the picture tends to be grainy and the colours washed out.

Furthermore, in low contrast situations, the camcorder's AF system might also encounter problems, which may mean you need to switch to manual focus. All these problems, however, can be solved by using add-on lights.

Some camcorders now come with lights built in, but accessory lights can be bought fairly cheaply. They give powerful illumination over a limited angle of view and can help pick out the subject from its background.

Set the white balance to the correct setting for the light. If you are shooting indoors, the light will drown out any tungsten or fluorescent lights when shining on the subject directly, so there should be no strange colour cast.

The problems with direct light are that harsh highlights can appear on the subject and, if the background is close, the subject can cast an unattractive shadow. To counter this, angle the light up, so it points at the ceiling halfway between the camcorder and subject.

Light is then 'bounced' off the ceiling to provide a diffused pool of light. This only works, however, if the ceiling is low enough and the light is powerful enough. Much of the light might otherwise be lost.

Tip: Which light?

Lights can be purchased from most shops that sell camcorders. They are very reasonably priced and can be attached to any camcorder with an accessory shoe.

Some lights are powered by the camcorder's battery, but the better ones have a rechargeable battery of their own, allowing much longer recording time.

The light here is a 'zoom light', which means the illumination can be altered between a powerful concentrated beam and a wider, less bright beam.

The narrow beam is used when you are shooting with the telephoto, and the wide beam when you are using the wide angle.

◀ ***When recording indoors, you have to decide which is the brightest – daylight coming through the windows or the illumination coming from the tungsten lights. If you use both, the white balance system is unable to cope. If the window light is brighter, position your subjects near to the window and turn down the tungsten lights.***

◀ ***If you use a camcorder-mounted video light, you don't need to worry about other light sources, as the video light will drown them out. However, the light can be very harsh and shadows may appear on the background.***

▼ ***Bouncing the light off the ceiling softens the light, making it look more natural. The colours are less accurate, as they will be tinted by the ceiling. This works best with powerful lights.***

Off camcorder lights

When using a camcorder light, you have to choose whether to shine the light directly at the subject (getting correct colour rendition, but very harsh highlights and deep shadows) or bouncing the light (for more even illumination, but unnatural colours).

As you become more advanced in your home movie making, you can light your subject using more powerful stand-alone lights. Of course, you have to be shooting at home, or in another location where you can set up the lights easily.

The subject, too, should be confined to one place, making it particularly useful for videoing interviews or people in conversation. This lighting set up is suited to those situations where the subject is looking at the camcorder or only slightly to one side.

When bouncing light, use a white ceiling, as most other colours absorb too much light. Choose a low ceiling, as high ceilings may reduce the light level too much.

Lamp attachments

Various attachments can be added to your video lamp to alter the quality and strength of the light.

Most lamps have **barndoors** attached to the front, which can be partially opened or closed to give a wide flood of light or a narrowed **spotlight**.

Snoots are conical funnels that attach to the front of the lamp to concentrate the beam of light. This creates a very bright spotlight for small areas.

To cut down the amount of light

1 THE KEY LIGHT
You should use your brightest light for this, as it is the main source of illumination on the subject. The power output of the light depends on how far away it is, and can vary from 100W to 1000W or even more if the lights are some distance away.

Place the light to one side of the camcorder, say between 25° and 45° to the side of the person's nose. This gives less harsh lighting than a front light mounted on the camcorder. However, it will give rise to deep shadows on the side of the face away from the light. Place the light higher than the subject, anywhere between 10° and 45° higher than the subject.

2 THE FILL LIGHT
The fill light also shines directly on the subject. Its job is to lift the shadows slightly, reducing the overall contrast on the face. However, it should not eliminate the shadows completely, as they help to give the face modelling.

You can achieve this by having a fill light that is lower powered than the key light. If you cannot adjust the power, place a diffuser in front of the light. It should be placed on the other side of the camcorder to the key light, but no more than 30° from the direction in which the subject is pointing.

further, a **flag** can be placed between the light beam and the subject. A flag is any piece of material through which light cannot pass, such as black card.

For more creative work, you can make a **gobo**. This is a piece of card or silver paper that has shapes cut out of it.

This enables you to project shapes such as a window frame at a wall. Waving strips of paper in front of a yellow/orange lamp can simulate firelight.

Although many video lights are balanced for daylight, some are more yellow. In this case, attach a blue **gel** over the lamp. Gels come in a variety of colours.

If direct light is too harsh, you can use indirect light. To do this, bounce the light from a video lamp off a light surface, such as a brolly or white card.

Alternatively, soften the light by placing a special flame-proof **diffuser** between the lamp and the subject. You can use tracing paper, but remember to hold it away from the light for safety.

▲ ***Most video lamps have barndoors fitted. Narrow the light beam by closing the barndoors slightly.***

3 THE BACKLIGHT

Although two lights may be enough, a third light is often introduced to separate the subject from their background. The backlight is again positioned above the subject, but behind and high up, say between 25° and 60° higher than the subject. This also adds an attractive halo to the subject's hair and shoulders.

4 THE SETTING LIGHT

A fourth light is the setting (background) light, for when the subject is close to the background. It helps brighten up the background and eliminate shadows cast by the key or fill lights. The setting light should have a wide beam, but none of its light should fall on the subject. A gobo (see Lamp attachments) can be placed over the light to create a background pattern. Here, for example, we shone the light through a tree.

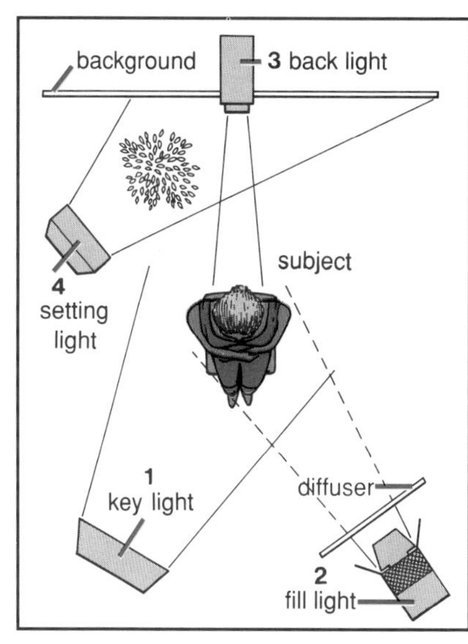

▲ ***The lights were switched on one by one. To obtain the mottled background, light 4 was shone through a tree.***

Natural sources

The principles of lighting apply whatever the light source. When you are outside, you can use the sun as your key light. Always check the position of the sun before you start to record.

If you shoot into the sun, your subject will be backlit. Not only will you have to open the iris or boost the gain to stop the subject from silhouetting, but the colours will look washed out.

If the sun is behind you, then the subject may be too harshly lit. If you are shooting people, they may also be tempted to squint.

So treat the sun as you would any other key light, and place it to the side of your subject, and slightly in front. However, as with a single video lamp, this may cause harsh shadows on the other side of the face.

Fill-in light

The solution is to add a fill light. This doesn't have to be an actual light, however, as a reflector will do equally well.

You can buy special reflectors, or you can make your own out of a piece of card. Leave one side white and cover the other with crumpled and unrolled silver foil.

Use the foil side in sunny conditions and the more reflective white side in dull overcast conditions. If space is limited, simply use a folded piece of foil.

If the sun is not visible in the sky, the contrast is likely to be low and the lighting good. However, for close-ups of faces, get somebody to hold a reflector below the person, reflecting light from the sky back into their face.

▲ ***When shooting in strong sunlight, you may encounter problems wherever the sun is with respect to your subject. If you place the sun behind them, they will be backlit, if you place the sun behind you, your subject will squint. Even if you place the sun to the side of your subject, you will get very harsh shadows on the side of the face that is away from the sun.***

▼ ***If you place a reflector to the side and slightly below the subject, you can reflect light back from the sun to the subject's face. This doesn't eliminate shadows completely – that would look unnatural. What it does is give a more even spread of light. You don't have to buy a special reflector – an unrolled piece of kitchen foil is just as good.***

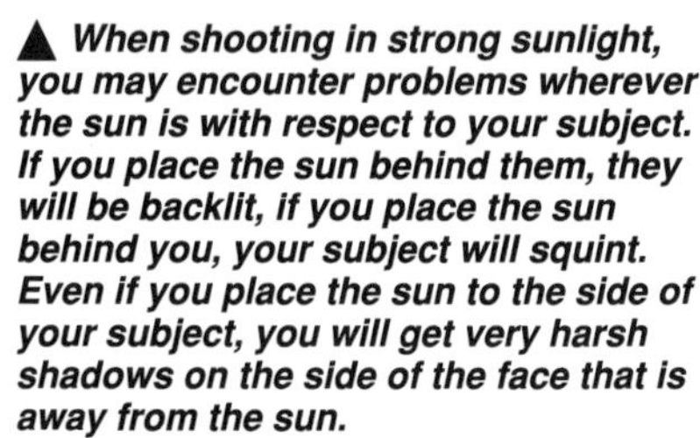

Tip

Light care

❑ Be careful when using video lights, as the bulbs can get very hot. Following long use, allow them to cool for ten minutes after switching them off before you try to move them.

❑ Don't touch the bulb with your bare hands, even when it's cold. Use gloves to prevent fingermarks – which greatly reduce bulb life.

❑ Any object placed in front of the light should be at least 10cm from the bulb.

❑ At all times, keep children away from the lamps.

❑ Tape any leads to the floor with masking tape so that nobody trips over them.

❑ Don't overload your circuit. If you are using a number of powerful lights, check with a qualified electrician first to see what is safe for your domestic wiring.

❑ If possible, monitor the shots at all times through a TV, as this will show you whether the exposure and white balance are correct.

Basic titling

Adding titles and captions is an easy way of making your videos look more professional, but there's an art to getting them right.

There are two methods of adding a title to your video. One is to generate it electronically and superimpose it over a shot. The other is to make your own title and then video it through the lens as you would any other subject.

The easiest way is to generate the titles electronically within the camcorder itself. For this you need a camcorder with either a character generator or title superimposer. Most camcorders have one or the other, and some have both.

Character generator With a character generator, you can create a title by typing in the individual letters using buttons on the camcorder. This method can be time consuming, as you have to run through the alphabet for each letter.

Optional extras

Some models have connections for credit card sized character generators with a mini keyboard built in. Once the title has been generated and positioned in the frame, it is stored in a digital memory.

When you reach the appropriate shot, simply press the 'recall' button and the title will be superimposed over the scene.

Title superimposers Some camcorders have these built in. They are quicker to use than character generators. To operate the title superimposer, simply point the camcorder at a scene and press the 'store' button.

The camcorder stores the dark parts of the image in a digital memory and ignores the lighter parts. This means that if you point it at a word or group of words written in a dark colour on white paper, it stores only the words.

The title is superimposed in the same way as a title created by a character generator. Simply press the superimpose button in the appropriate scene.

Some camcorders have two digital memories, so you can store two titles. If you know what titles you are likely to use, store them first, so you don't have to waste time creating them at the time of shooting.

If your camcorder has a title superimposer, write the titles beforehand and carry them with you. Leave plenty of white space around the title, so that you can position it anywhere appropriate on the screen.

title generator

◀▼▲ ***First create a title by using the camcorder's character generator or title superimposer. When it is stored in the memory, select the scene over which you want to place the title and press the superimpose button.***

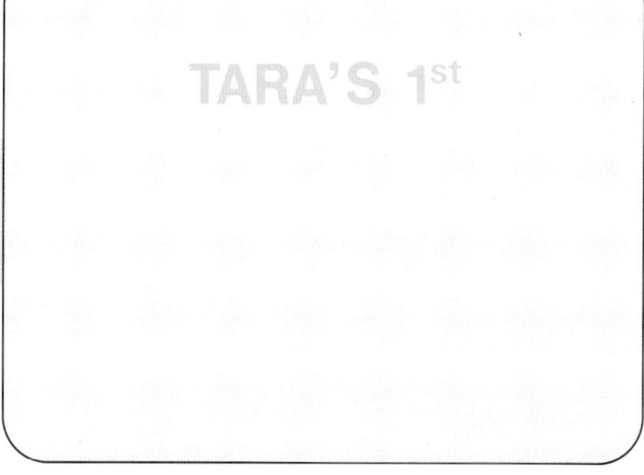

Creating captions

When you create electronic titles using a title superimposer, you have to create the title first, then store it in the memory.

If you are not too concerned with appearance, you can simply write on a piece of paper in pen. However, if the lines are too thin, the image will break up.

The best thing to do is to use transfer letters or a thick felt pen and stencils. When choosing a typeface, go for a bold face, rather than a slender one, as it will be a lot easier to read on-screen.

Always use black lettering on a white background, as this gives the boldest title. Title superimposers give you the option of changing the colour of the title in-camera.

When selecting the appropriate colour, don't choose one that is similar to the colour of the background. More importantly, if the background is light, choose a dark title and vice versa.

▲ *Place your titles in an uncluttered part of the picture, avoiding the edge of the frame.*

Mono advantage

This is one area where black and white viewfinders are useful, because they show differences in tone. If the title is easy to read in the viewfinder, it should be clearly visible on the screen.

Choose a background that is uncluttered. Ideally, find one that has a large area of the same colour – such as sky or grass – and superimpose the title over that.

Keep the titles short, and large enough to be easily read. Leave them on the screen for at least as long as it takes to read them twice to yourself.

Words entirely in capital letters have greater impact, but are not so easy to read as non-capital letters. If you have a number of words – because you are adding a subtitle, for instance – don't use capitals. For one or two words, however, capitals may look better.

Place subtitles at the bottom of the frame. However, make sure you are using a colour that stands out from the background. When positioning the title don't use the outer 10-15% of the screen, as some of the lettering may be lost when you replay the recording on your tv screen.

Whenever you are adding titles, it is vital that you keep the camcorder steady the whole time, so fix the title firmly in one position and place the camcorder on a tripod or other firm base.

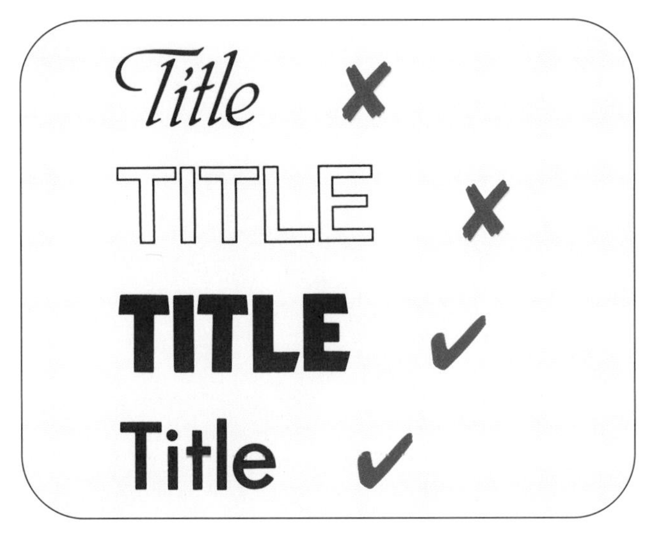

▼ *Use typefaces that are solid. For one or two words, capitals have more impact, but non-capital letters are easier to read.*

▼ *Choose a colour that contrasts with the background. Tone is also important – if the background is light, the lettering should be dark.*

Making your own

You don't have to generate titles electronically. If your camcorder doesn't have any titling facility, or if you simply feel like being a bit more creative, you can create physical titles and shoot them.

The easiest way of creating this kind of title is to stick white lettering on to a dark background. You can select different coloured lettering, but keep it plain.

If you want to be really creative, you can use appropriate props to create the title. If you wanted to shoot an opening title for a holiday video, for instance, you might write the title in pebbles or shells on the beach.

If you time your shooting correctly, you might even be able to get the tide to wash over it. This kind of creative title can be used again and again. Once the wave has washed over the title, you can pause the camcorder and set up the next title. Use the wide angle end of the lens to avoid camera shake.

▲▶ ***Although camcorders allow you to create electronic titles, you can be far more artistic with physical titles. The titles here – for a wedding and a country walk – are far more sophisticated than anything the camcorder could produce. Make sure the title card and the camcorder are securely fixed before you start to record.***

Creative captions

Alternatively, show items that are connected with the event you are videoing. For instance, if you are filming a wedding, you could shoot a wedding invitation and a champagne glass or bouquet. The writing on the invitation would serve as a caption.

Similarly, for a birthday party, you can use the writing on the cake – especially if the name is spelt out in candles. Whatever form your title is in, remember to keep it level by using a tripod if possible.

If you want to show a series of titles that are, say, white on black, you can set the camcorder on a tripod and point it at the first title. Start recording and, after a few seconds, fade down the picture. Pause and fade up to reveal the next title.

Easy titles

Dedicated video title boards, such as this 'Easy Titler' are also available for creative captioning.

This one consists of a metal board and magnetic letters that can be arranged on the board to spell out the title you require.

Different backgrounds, such as those used for silent film captions, are also included to give the title a more creative feel.

Set the camcorder on a book or desktop tripod when using title boards to avoid shake.

Editing in titles

Shooting a video is a lot easier if you allow yourself the luxury of editing it later. Similarly, although it may be time-consuming, adding titles while editing can save you a lot of hassle at the shooting stage.

Your camcorder may allow you to create and add titles while copying, but if not, you need an add-on caption generator. Some advanced editing units have caption generators built in.

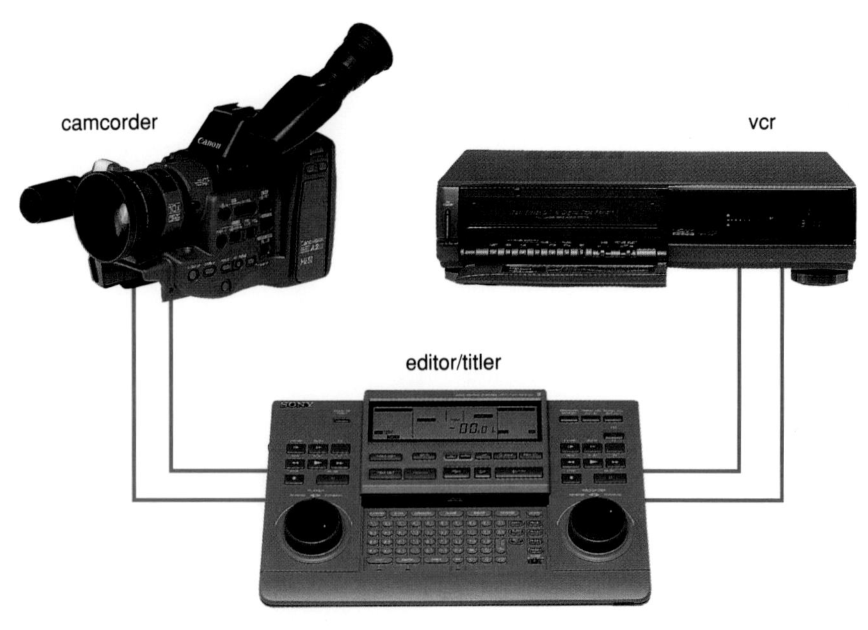

▲ ***Connect the camcorder to the titler and the titler to the video recorder. Add the titles while copying the shots during editing.***

Key advantages

A titler works in the same way as an on-camcorder title generator. Most have good-sized keyboards built in, and some of the more sophisticated allow you to scroll the titles up, down or in from the side. Some even allow you to zoom into the title until it fills the frame.

A choice of colours and typefaces is available, and titles can be positioned at the most appropriate place in the shot.

Once you have stored your titles, connect the *video out* from the camcorder to the *video in* on the titler and the *video out* from the titler to the *video in* on the VCR. The audio lead can run through the titler or from camcorder to VCR.

You then simply copy the tape from camcorder to VCR as you would normally. Whenever a shot is being copied that you want to insert a title over, simply press the superimpose button and the title will appear on the VCR tape.

How to add titles

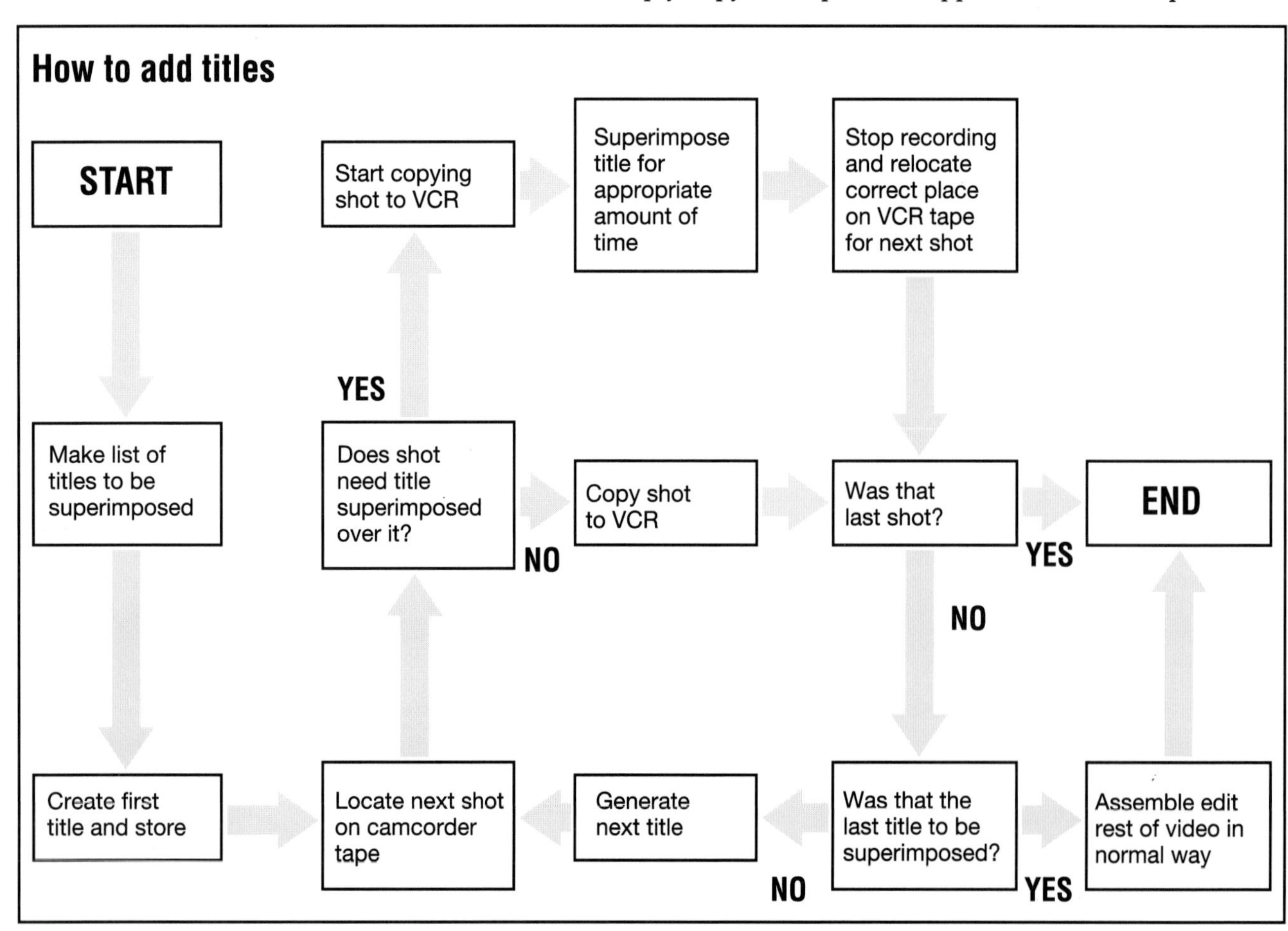

Putting it all together

If you find watching your recordings is less exciting than shooting them, it may be that they could benefit from a spot of editing.

You can play back your recordings by connecting the camcorder to the TV. It is also possible to copy the video on to a blank VHS tape by connecting your camcorder to the VCR. (But remember it's illegal to copy feature films.)

There are three reasons why you would want to copy your video:

❑ **To change format** to VHS. This enables you to play back your tape without having to unpack your camcorder. You can also lend the copy to anyone with a VCR.

❑ **To add commentary** or music to the copy tape while you are copying. This can make your videos sound more professional.

❑ **To change what you've shot** as you copy – the most important reason of all.

In-camera editing

Advice on thinking shots through before starting to record and planning your sequences before you shoot was given on pages 39-42.

If you follow this method you are selecting – editing – your material as you shoot. This is known as in-camera editing.

With in-camera editing, you don't need to do anything else to your video after you've shot it. You can simply play it back as it stands.

Relying on this method can be a bit limiting. You have to judge the right length for each shot while you're shooting, and make sure that everything is in the order you want it to appear on the video.

Copying from one tape to another gives you the flexibility to change the length of your shots and the order in which they appear.

When you play back your video, you might find some of the shots are longer than you remember and could do with trimming. Some shots might have technical problems, or the camera may have been recording when you thought it was paused. You can get rid of the bad shots by simply missing them out when you copy.

UNEDITED SEQUENCE

1

2

3

4

5

6

EDITED SEQUENCE

2

▲ ***A nice shot of children playing. However, before it on the tape is a shot of the camera operator's feet – an example of leaving the camcorder recording when you thought it was paused. Miss this shot out and start the video with the second shot.***

4

▲ ***A shot of an adult watching the children. However, there's a technical fault at the start. Perhaps the camera was left in manual focus and had to be switched back to autofocus. Miss out the bad bit of the shot.***

6

▲ ***Nothing wrong with this shot, except that it goes on for too long. You can shorten the length of the shot by copying only as much of it as you think it warrants. Miss out the bit with the least activity.***

▲ UNEDITED SEQUENCE
The four shots in the order they were recorded. Part of the show is recorded first, and the cameraman then turns the camcorder on various members of the crowd. Finally, he looks round for a good establishing shot, which he shoots from the balcony of a nearby wine bar.

Rearranging the shots

Copying from tape to tape offers more advantages than cutting out errors. It also allows you to rearrange the shots in a more logical or interesting order.

This is a more advanced – but by no means more complicated – method of approaching video. It involves shooting all the shots you need, then assembling them in the right order when you copy. This process is called assemble editing.

Assemble editing

Although it sounds like more work, assemble editing actually makes shooting your video easier. It allows you to hold shots for a lot longer than you normally would, as you can cut out everything you don't want later.

It also means you can shoot interesting subjects as they happen, without worrying about whether they are in the right order on the tape. They can be rearranged later during assemble edit.

Another advantage is that you can compile a video made up of events shot at completely different times. For instance, if you missed an establishing shot to show where an event takes place, you can record it at a different time and drop it into the copy tape at the appropriate point.

Programme length

Assemble editing is the key to creating interesting videos. If you video an event, you may have over an hour of material in a fairly random order.

This can be edited down to a well ordered 15-20 minutes, and could make the difference between a video people want to watch and

▼ EDITED SEQUENCE
The bottom sequence shows the same shots rearranged in a more logical order, with the establisher at the beginning and the shots of Punch & Judy separated by a shot of the spectators. Assemble edit makes such shot rearrangement possible.

one where their attention wanders.

You have to judge the length of each shot yourself, but don't bore your audience – err on the side of shortness.

Hold static shots for just long enough for the viewer to take in the information. With assemble editing, you can try a number of different lengths until you find the one that works best.

When you want the viewer to read something on the screen, such as a sign or title, hold the shot for a bit longer than it takes you to read it yourself. This gives people time to digest the information and allows for slow readers.

You can also reinforce the pace of fast action subjects by using a series of short shots. It is a lot easier to judge the best length for a shot during assemble edit than when shooting.

Moving shots should be held for a second or two at the end. This includes pans, tilts and zooms.

When panning or tilting, hold a static shot for a couple of seconds before you start the movement. This is not necessary with zooms, as it is acceptable to start the shot while zooming.

Speech recording

Assemble editing can solve the problem of not knowing when to end a shot of somebody making a speech or telling a joke.

When you edit in-camera, you might cut somebody off before they've finished talking, or keep recording them beyond the interesting part of their speech.

If you assemble edit, keep recording until you are sure there's nothing more. Copy just the best bits later.

Assemble edit – step by step

1 LOG YOUR SHOTS
Before you assemble edit, note down all the shots on your tape and the position of the tape counter at the start of each shot. Rewrite the list in the order you want them to appear. This is called logging your shots, and it makes finding the next shot to copy a lot easier.

2 SET UP YOUR EQUIPMENT
Connect your camcorder, video recorder and television together using the method explained in your camcorder's instruction manual. You can then monitor what is being recorded on the television.

3 LINE UP THE FIRST SHOT
Check your log sheet to see which is the first shot you want to record.

4 PREPARE THE VCR
Find the point on the video recorder tape where you want to begin the shot and pause the video in record/pause mode.

5 PREPARE THE CAMCORDER
Play the camcorder tape until about a second before the point where you want the shot to start, and pause.

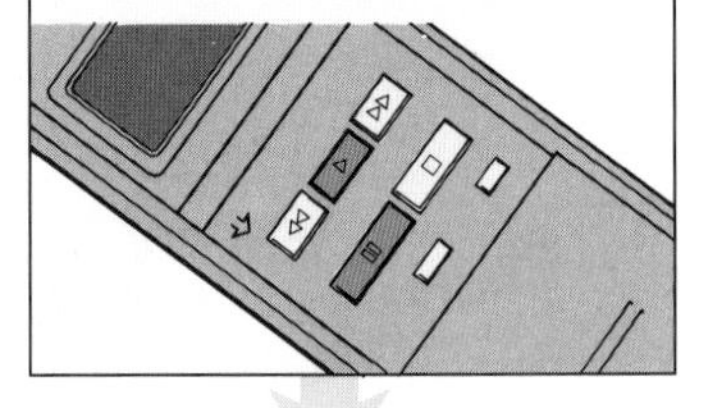

6 RECORD THE SHOT
Release both pause buttons at the same time. This records the first shot on to the video recorder tape.

7 MONITOR THE RECORDING
Watch the recording being made on the television and let it run on for a couple of seconds after the shot has finished.

8 CHECK THE RECORDING
Rewind the recording tape and play back the shot. Has it recorded successfully?

NO → **RE-RECORD SHOT**

YES →

9 CHECK LOG SHEET
Was that the last shot?

NO →

10 RECORD NEXT SHOT
Cross off the shot you've recorded on your log sheet and move to next shot.

YES →

END

Tip: Quality counts

If you're planning to assemble edit your videos, it's best to use S-VHS or Hi8, and record in standard play mode on pro-grade tape.

Every time you copy from one tape to another, the quality of the copy is reduced, so you need to start with top quality. The soundtrack can become less distinct, while areas of the picture can break up.

You only have to copy once to make your master recording, but if anybody wants a copy of the finished video, you have to record from the master.

With standard VHS and 8mm, this copy of a copy can be of significantly poorer quality than the original, particularly if the recording is made in long play mode.

Just a second?

The extra second has been included to make up for the fact that the video recorder rewinds over about this much tape before it starts to record. It does this for technical reasons that ensure there is a clean edit between each shot.

This is known as 'roll-back', and it can vary from machine to machine, from about half a second to as much as three seconds, so do a few test runs with your video recorder first to check the exact length.

A far more accurate method is to use specially designed editing equipment, which we look at next.

Editing equipment

If you intend to edit your videos extensively, there are a number of pieces of equipment designed to make the process easier.

▲ ***Some VCRs are better for editing than others. Most models have a backspacing facility for clean edits. Look for good A/V inputs and outputs and a jog/shuttle dial. If you have a hi-band camcorder, an S-VHS VCR gives optimum picture quality. For top sound quality look for a hi-fi Nicam deck.***

Assemble editing is an extension of copying. The only difference is that editing involves selection. You choose the shots you want, and the order in which you want them.

Every time you transfer a shot from one tape to another, you have to find the exact place on both the camcorder and the VCR tape where you want the shot to start.

This can be time-consuming. However, equipment is available to make the task easier. First is your choice of VCR. You can copy to any VCR with backspacing facility, as described on the previous few pages, but not all have the same sockets.

All VCRs have aerial ('RF') inputs and outputs. You can connect the camcorder to the VCR via RF, but you won't end up with optimum quality.

The best method is to use direct inputs ('A/V' leads). This gives much better picture and sound quality than using RF. Camcorders have separate audio and video outputs (usually 'phono' plugs), which can be connected to the A/V inputs of your VCR. Most VCRs have an A/V input – either phono sockets or a 21-pin 'Scart' socket.

Jog/shuttle

The best VCRs have two Scart sockets – one to receive the signal from the camcorder, the other to output the signal to the TV.

You get the best quality when using an S-VHS or Hi8 camcorder. Run the signal from the camcorder's S-video output to the VCR's Scart socket or S-terminal.

The other useful feature on a VCR is a jog/shuttle – a large central knob on the front panel of the machine. A jog/shuttle enables you to review the picture on the tape one frame at a time.

This makes cueing up the VCR tape a lot easier, cutting the time it takes to edit your video. If you record from one VCR to another, the ideal situation is to have a jog/shuttle on both.

TV times two

When you record from camcorder to VCR, the TV shows what is playing on the VCR if it is in PLAY or PLAY/PAUSE mode. It shows the camcorder tape if the VCR is in RECORD or RECORD/PAUSE mode.

Although you only need one TV, there are advantages in having two. The second TV should be arranged so that it always shows what is on the camcorder tape. This enables you to see where you have paused the camcorder tape when you are cueing the VCR tape.

There are three ways of connecting the second TV to your equipment:

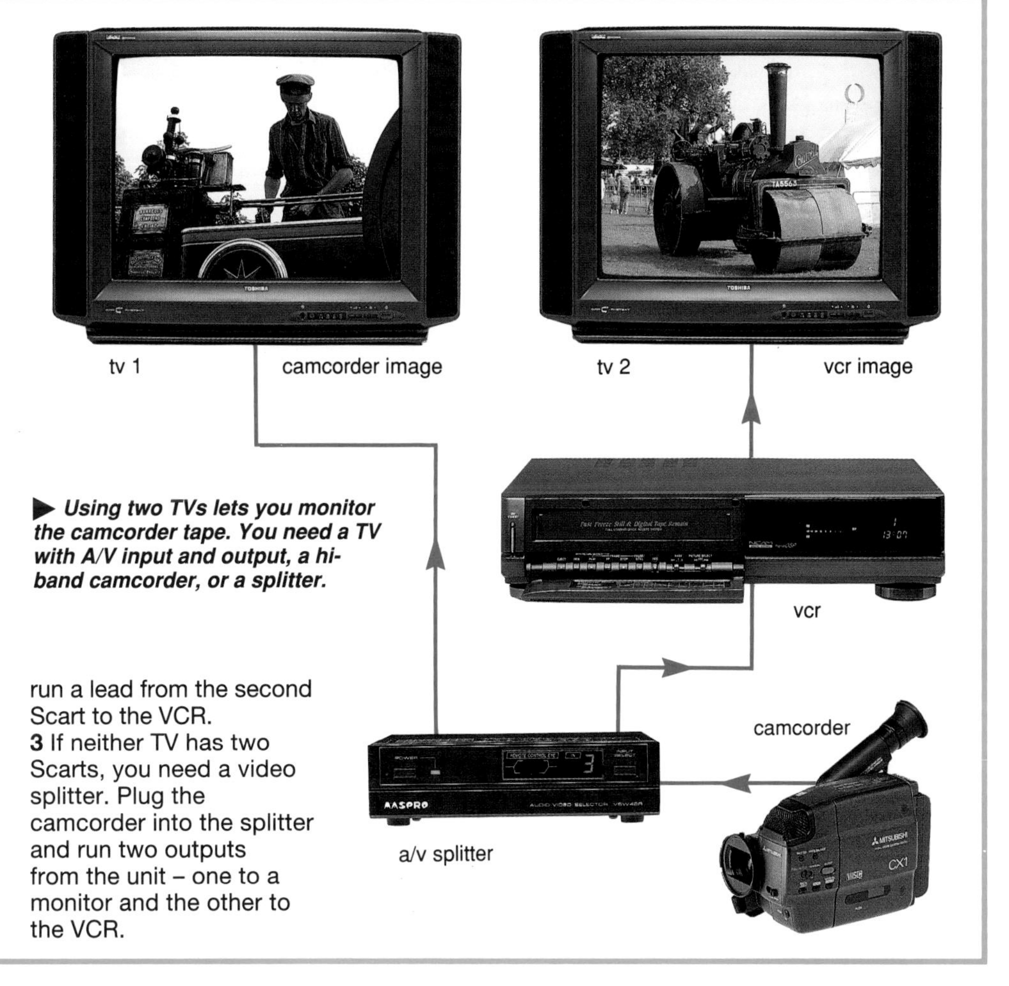

▶ ***Using two TVs lets you monitor the camcorder tape. You need a TV with A/V input and output, a hi-band camcorder, or a splitter.***

1 If you have a Hi8 or S-VHS camcorder, you have two outputs (phono sockets and an S-socket). Run the output from one to the first monitor and the other to the VCR.

2 If you have a TV with two Scarts, run the camcorder output to one of them, and run a lead from the second Scart to the VCR.

3 If neither TV has two Scarts, you need a video splitter. Plug the camcorder into the splitter and run two outputs from the unit – one to a monitor and the other to the VCR.

Synchro-editing

One of the biggest problems with editing is the accuracy of the cut. Sometimes, the cut can be a second or more away from the point where you wanted it.

This may be because of the difficulty of pressing the camcorder and VCR pause buttons in unison, or it may be because of the equipment's 'roll-back' time (see 'Just a second?' on page 72).

The most basic method the manufacturers have devised for making editing more accurate is 'synchro-editing'. As well as connecting the camcorder to the VCR via the A/V leads, you can also connect them via a synchro-edit lead.

Not all camcorders and video recorders can be connected via a synchro-edit lead. First, both pieces of equipment need a synchro-edit socket (normally only found on better quality VCRs), and second, the two units have to be made by the same manufacturer.

Synchro-editing gives two main advantages. First, once you have paused the camcorder and VCR at the right point, touching the pause button on the VCR starts the VCR recording and the camcorder playing, so you don't have to try and press them at the same time.

Second, because manufacturers know the roll-back times of their own pieces of equipment, they can delay the signal to the video recorder by the roll-back time to give greater editing accuracy.

▲ Synchro-editing is simple and inexpensive – so long as you have a camcorder and video recorder from the same company and with the right connections. It allows you to operate the video recorder and camcorder from one set of controls and provides fairly accurate edits.

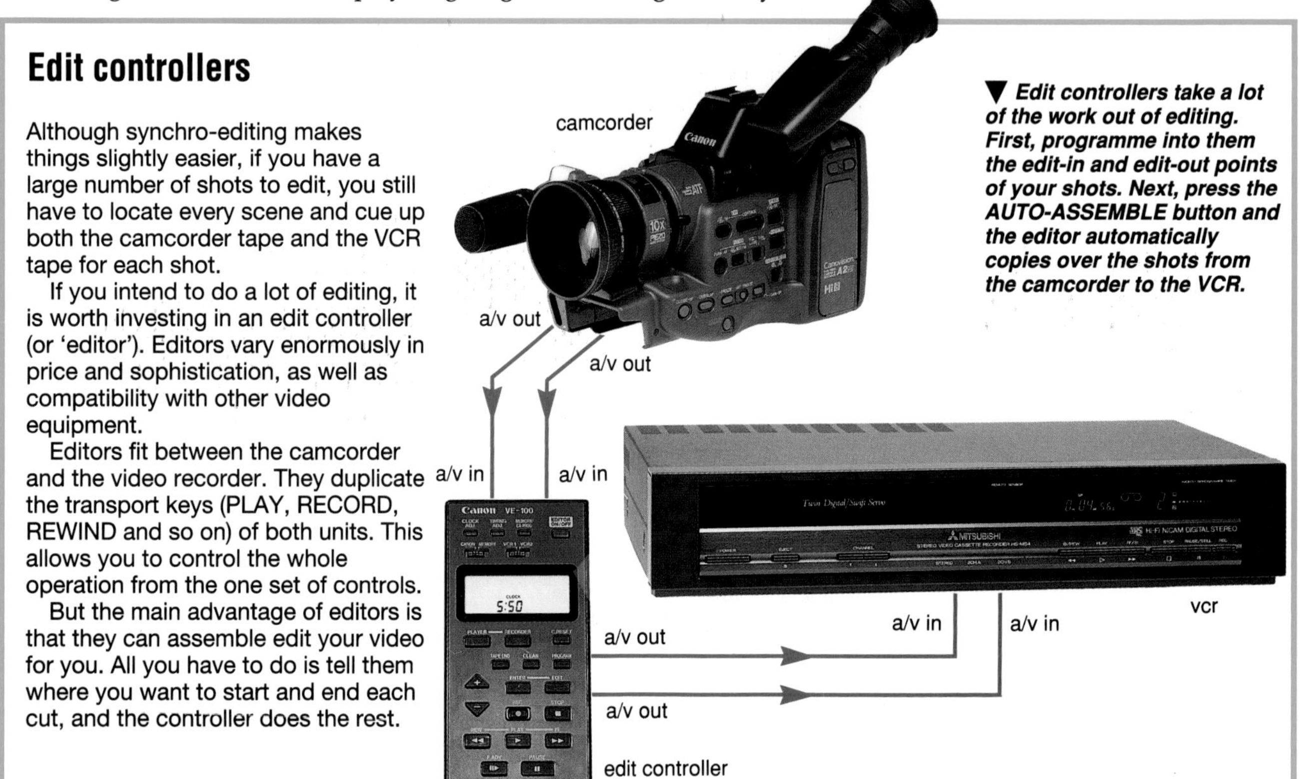

Edit controllers

Although synchro-editing makes things slightly easier, if you have a large number of shots to edit, you still have to locate every scene and cue up both the camcorder tape and the VCR tape for each shot.

If you intend to do a lot of editing, it is worth investing in an edit controller (or 'editor'). Editors vary enormously in price and sophistication, as well as compatibility with other video equipment.

Editors fit between the camcorder and the video recorder. They duplicate the transport keys (PLAY, RECORD, REWIND and so on) of both units. This allows you to control the whole operation from the one set of controls.

But the main advantage of editors is that they can assemble edit your video for you. All you have to do is tell them where you want to start and end each cut, and the controller does the rest.

▼ Edit controllers take a lot of the work out of editing. First, programme into them the edit-in and edit-out points of your shots. Next, press the AUTO-ASSEMBLE button and the editor automatically copies over the shots from the camcorder to the VCR.

Automatic assembly

Editors can store the start and end point of a number of shots. The most basic can cope with only a handful, but some of the more sophisticated can store around 100.

To use an editor, play your camcorder tape until you get to the point where you want the first shot to start. Press the CUT IN (or equivalent) button on the editor.

Shuttle forward until you reach the point where you want the shot to end and press the CUT OUT button on the editor. Repeat this for as many shots as the editor allows you to assemble in one go.

When you finish programming the cuts, press AUTO-ASSEMBLE. This controls both camcorder and video recorder, assembling the shots automatically.

The most basic editors work by storing the tape counter number at the edit points you've chosen. You can see the tape counter (in hours, minutes and seconds) in your camcorder's viewfinder.

Although editors take the labour out of editing, they can be unpredictable. If the tape is constantly being wound forwards and backwards, clock errors may begin to creep in. This can lead to inaccurate cuts – often getting more inaccurate as the assembly process continues. Total accuracy is not possible.

Tip

Pick your model

Not all editors work with all camcorders and VCRs. Editors from 8mm manufacturers generally only work with 8mm camcorders. Editors made by VHS manufacturers only work with VHS/VHS-C camcorders.

This is because the connections carrying the counter information from camcorder to editor are different for the two formats.

Compatibility between editor and VCR is easier, as the editor controls the VCR via infra-red remote control, so virtually all VCRs are compatible. Editors made by independent accessory companies often have connections for both 8mm and VHS camcorders.

IN 1

This is the point at which you want to start recording the first shot. Forward the camcorder tape to this point and press the CUT-IN button.

OUT 1

Let the shot play until you get to the point where you want it to end. Press the CUT-OUT button on the edit controller.

IN 2

Cue the camcorder tape to the point where you want the second shot to start. Press the CUT-IN on the editor.

OUT 2

When you get to the point where you want the second shot to end press the CUT-OUT button. When you have programmed in as many shots as you want, press the AUTO-ASSEMBLE button and the editor will do all the work for you.

Time-coding

Not all editors work by reading the counter pulse off the camcorder. More sophisticated machines use a far more accurate method called 'time-code'.

Time-code editors are the cream of the editing devices. They work by reading a code that is laid on the tape, so they are not thrown if the tape mechanism slips a few seconds.

Time-codes not only read hours, minutes and seconds, but frames too. Each of the 25 frames has its own unique code.

Counter reading and time-code reading editors work in the same way – you select the cut in and cut out points and the editor assembles the video automatically. The only difference is that time-code editors are ideally accurate to a frame, although small backspacing errors can still creep in.

This allows you to cut with precision – important if you are rapidly cutting between shots that only last for a few seconds. If you are only editing to get rid of the spoilt footage (shots of your feet and so on), time-code accuracy is not essential.

▲ ***Time code generators write an individual label on every frame. This can be 'read' by the editor, but does not appear on the picture when you copy it on to the video recorder tape.***

Which system?

The time-code editing market is a confusing one because there are currently two incompatible systems: VITC ('vitsee' – vertical integrated time-code) and RCTC ('arctic' rewritable consumer time-code).

VITC is used by VHS manufacturers. Its advantage is that, for a selected number of camcorders, you can buy a cheap VITC writer which lays the time-code on the tape at the time of recording.

If you want to add VITC to a pre-recorded tape, you have to copy it on to another tape and add the time-code then. This means you have to lose a generation of quality just to add VITC.

RCTC – the 8mm system – has the advantage that it can be added to a tape after it has been recorded. The disadvantage is that you have to have a camcorder with a built-in RCTC generator to use it.

▶ ***Two types of time-code editing units help accurate edits. VITC (used with VHS equipment) (top) is added to the tape while the shot is being recorded or copied. RCTC (for the 8mm system) (bottom) can be added to the tape at any time, without affecting the picture.***

The right cut

When cutting between two shots in a sequence, choosing the right position to move to, and the right moment to cut, can help hide the edit point.

If you expand your videomaking so that you shoot scripted material, one of the most common scenes you can shoot is two people talking to each other. The method normally employed for such exchanges is the 'shot/reverse shot' convention.

According to the convention, when you cut between two people having a conversation, you should match the angles of the eyelines between them. The main consideration is that if one person is facing towards the right of the screen, the other should face the left.

The next thing to look out for is if the two people are at different heights. Lower or raise the camera so that it is at the same height as each person, but if one is looking down by, say, 30°, the other must look up by 30°.

The degree of 'frontality' – whether they are seen in profile, facing the camera or at any point in between – should be the same for both people. If one person is facing 45° to the front left, the other person should be facing 45° to the front right.

The greater the degree of frontality (the more directly the actors are facing the camera) the more dramatic the exchange. For everyday conversations you should choose a low degree of frontality. If, however, you want the conversation to be confrontational, you can shoot an 'over the shoulder' shot, which includes both people.

One thing that doesn't have to be the same for both people is the shot size. If one is more important, because they are being interviewed or because they are saying something important, they should be shown larger than the other.

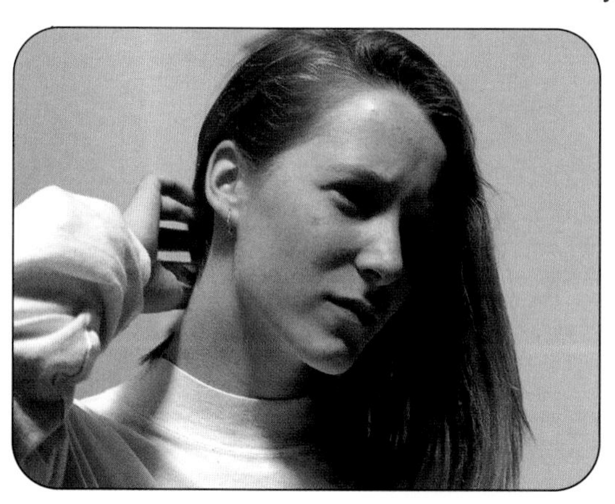

◀ ***The person on the left is standing and so is higher than the person on the right. To reflect this, move the camcorder down to the height of the person on the right and tilt the camcorder up slightly.***

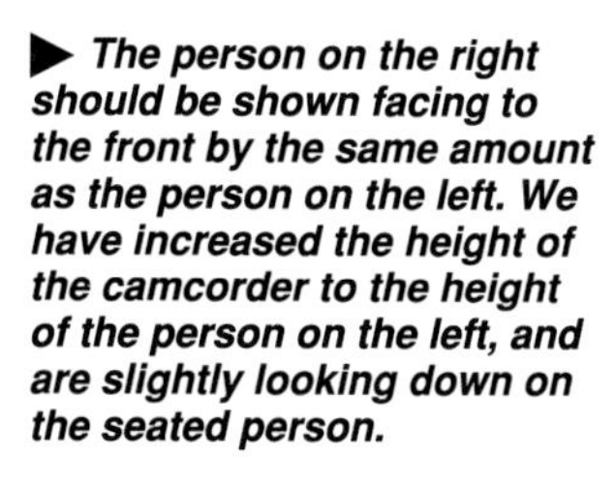

▶ ***The person on the right should be shown facing to the front by the same amount as the person on the left. We have increased the height of the camcorder to the height of the person on the left, and are slightly looking down on the seated person.***

The set up

For shooting a conversation of this kind, it is best to record the scene twice – with the camcorder framing just one of the people in each 'take'. However, the subjects must perform the scene identically.

An alternative is to find somebody else with a camcorder and shoot the scene using both. With either method you can edit the shots together later.

It is usual to show the person talking, but if the other's reaction is more interesting – say, if the conversation concerns them personally – it may be more interesting to show them reacting.

At the beginning and end of the scene, you can also have an establishing shot, consisting of a scene showing both subjects.

Cutting on action

▲ ***These two sequences (A1 to A4 and B1 to B4) represent two shots of the same subject. A1 takes place at the same time as B1, and A2 at the same time as B2. A1 takes place a second before A2 and two seconds before A3. The action has been recorded twice. We have to decide at which point we should end shot A and at which point we should start shot B.***

We have seen that if you change the shot size and angle correctly between two shots of the same subject, you can avoid a jump cut and help hide the edit. But there are also better moments to cut if you want to make the cut invisible.

The most frequently used method is called 'cutting on action'. According to this convention, if you cut while someone is performing an action, such as standing up, lifting a glass or reaching out to open a door, the action helps to hide the cut.

Cutting on action works – the only problem is that the timing of the cut has to be perfect. This is where time-code editing units (see **Video** Editing equipment) come into their own, as they ensure frame accuracy.

The above sequences show portions of two shots of the same action, taken from different positions. The action was performed identically in both shots.

Each of the stills represents a second further on in the action. Shots A1 and B1 take place a second into the action, shots A2 and B2 two seconds and so on. Rather than shooting someone talking to camera in one shot, make it more interesting by cutting out natural pauses. Get the speaker to end a shot by turning their head.

Pause the camcorder and move to the position they are now facing. Ask them to repeat the turn at the start of the next shot.

Action cut

A1 → A2 → A3 A4

↓

B1 B2 B3 → B4

Right. The best moment to cut is during the action, which takes place around the third second. When editing, record as far as the third second of the shot A and from the third second of the shot B.

Condensing time

A1 A2 A3 A4

↘

B1 B2 → B3 → B4

Acceptable. It is possible to condense time when cutting by missing out an unimportant piece of the shot. Here, we are cutting shot A after one second and starting shot B two seconds in.

As there is no action in shot B between seconds one and two, it is safe to cut out a second. However, the cut is not as neat as when you cut on action.

Double action

A1 → A2 → A3   A4

B1   B2 → B3 → B4

Wrong. One of the biggest problems you can encounter when attempting to cut on action is showing the action twice. By ending shot A after three seconds, but starting shot B after only two, the arm movement appears twice.

Missing action

A1 → A2   A3   A4

B1   B2   B3 → B4

Wrong. The opposite problem to double action can occur when some important action is missed out during the cut. By ending shot A two seconds in and starting shot B three seconds in, we go from the person having their hand on the bar to the glass being raised to their lips. The important arm movement is missed out.

Delayed cut

A1 → A2 → A3 → A4

B1   B2   B3   B4

Acceptable. By cutting after the action, you miss the opportunity to hide the cut – only acceptable if shot B runs on after B4. Similar is an 'early cut', where you cut shot A after one second and start shot B after one second. Both look untidy on screen.

Continuity of appearance

The other problem in cutting between shots of the same subject is that either the subject's appearance changes or the two takes of the action differ.

Continuity errors of the first kind often occur because the subject takes off a jacket or scarf between takes. Fast-changing objects, such as drinks and cigarettes, can also cause problems. (Humphrey Bogart is famous for having a cigarette that constantly expanded and shrunk during a scene.)

Continuity errors of the second kind could occur in the above sequence if the person uses their right hand to reach for the door in shot A and their left hand in shot B. Using two camcorders can solve these continuity problems.

Cutaways

Shots that deal with the main action in your video are known as 'master shots'. Most shots in video are master shots, but there are other kinds that can be extremely useful in certain situations.

We have already come across the establishing shot, which helps to locate where the action takes place. A third kind of shot is the 'cutaway'. Cutaways are immensely useful for the home movie editor.

Any shot that is not part of the main action, but is of an incidental event related to the action, is a cutaway. Cutaways add interest to a video, but more importantly they help to condense time, as well as acting as 'video plasters' that can help smooth over bad edits.

For instance, if you were videoing the highlights of a soccer game, every time you paused the camcorder and started a new shot, it is highly likely that anyone watching will notice that the ball and players are on different parts of the pitch from an instant before.

◀ ***The camcorder was paused between shots of the tiger. However, every time we pause the camcorder, a jump appears in the action. We have to find some way of 'plastering' over the cracks so that the viewer doesn't notice the edit points.***

▲◀ ***By inserting a cutaway between the two master shots of the tiger, we hide the fact that there has been a jump in the action. You can shoot cutaways at any time and edit them in at the appropriate point by copying to your VCR tape.***

Seconds count

However, if you were to insert a cutaway between the two master shots of the game, for instance a shot of somebody in the crowd waving a scarf, you would disguise the fact that play has moved on. A cutaway need only last for a second or two to be effective.

Some cutaways convey important information themselves. For instance, for a sports game, a shot of a scoreboard not only helps hide the edit point, but also provides important information.

Similarly, shots of objects that are referred to by speakers, or the reactions of listeners, also make good cutaways. Others, such as the slow zoom out from a bird sitting on the pitch or a person in the crowd eating a sandwich, simply provide visual interest.

The other useful purpose that cutaways serve is to hide any cuts that might otherwise jar the viewer. Cutaways can be used to disguise both jump cuts and instances where the camcorder has crossed the line of action (see **Between the shots**, page 43).

If you recorded a shot of a person telling a joke, then paused the camcorder for a minute before recording again from the same spot, you would get a jump cut. If you inserted a cutaway between the two shots, however, there would be no jump.

Big breaks

Although cutaways are often close-ups of people or objects, there is no reason why they can't be any shot size. In fact, establishing shots showing the entire location can also make good cutaways.

Like establishing shots, it is good to shoot a lot of cutaways. Close-ups of people applauding are fairly universal, and may be dropped into a number of situations – even if they were not shot in the same location as the master shot.

Similarly, an attractive sunset can be inserted into a number of videos to convey the end of the day. If it is followed by a daytime shot, we know the action has moved on to next morning.

Applied video – The sports match

Videoing sports matches is one of the most popular activities in video. The trick is to realize your limitations and produce a short video of edited highlights.

Sports matches and television go together so well that many people are more used to seeing sports matches on TV than seeing them live. But so that the coverage looks professional, TV companies often have half a dozen or more cameras, placed in the best positions around the ground.

If the match is being shown live, all the cameras are fed into a device called a production switcher. The view from each camera is shown on a different TV monitor, and the production crew constantly switch between the cameras to show the best view of the action. A special video recorder is set up to play back action replays. With recorded matches, the only difference is that the production team has slightly more time.

When you record a sports match with one camcorder, you can't possibly obtain all the views that a professional TV crew can. But the task is not too difficult – so long as you realize your limitations.

The easy way of recording a sports match is to keep the camcorder in one position. Ideally, you should look down slightly on the action, so you can see over the players' heads. The camcorder should also be mounted on a tripod.

The problem with this easy approach is that the same camera position throughout can make a boring video and create 'jump cuts'. In addition, by only shooting from one spot, you may miss action that is obscured by other players.

Following the ball

The best way of shooting a football match is to aim for a video showing highlights of the match, rather than the full 90 minutes. This makes the game not only easier to shoot, but also more watchable.

Take advantage of quiet moments in the game to move to another position. For instance, if a corner is being taken, you should quickly move to the far side of the goal and set up your camcorder.

It is not practical to move your tripod around with you, but as you will be using the telephoto lens to crop in close to the action, there is a risk of camera shake. The solution is to use a monopod.

This not only steadies the camcorder, but also bears much of the weight. However, don't worry unduly about camera shake, as it is less noticeable when the camcorder is moving rapidly to follow action.

The other essential item of kit is a spare battery. As you can't reshoot anything, there is no need to review what you've shot, so this should save power.

▲ ***A monopod is a perfect accessory for sports matches. It lends support, and is easy to carry from one position to another.***

◀ ***Throughout most of the match, you will be trying to capture good action shots, which means following the ball as much as possible. Although you need to crop in on the action, don't move in so tight that you can't follow the ball easily.***

Line of action

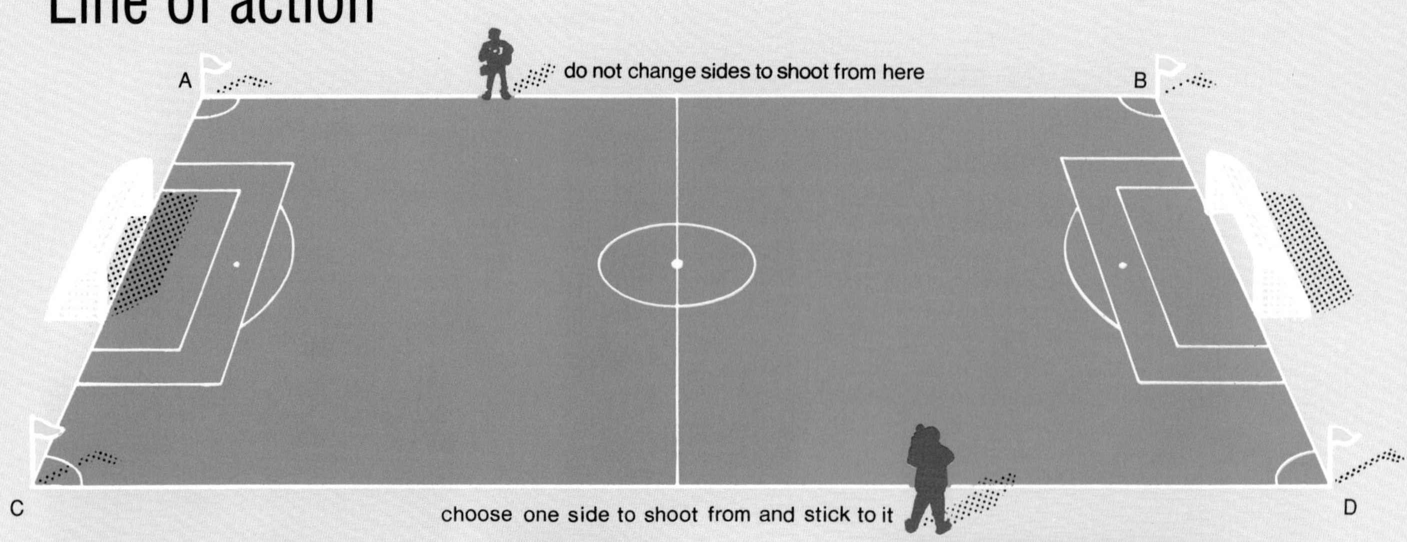

Although you should move from position to position when shooting a football match, there are better places to shoot from than others. The aim is not to confuse the viewer by crossing from one side of a moving subject to another when you cut. If you do, the subject appears to change directions between shots (see **Between the shots**, page 43).

The same problem occurs when shooting a football match. Imagine recording a shot from line CD on the above diagram. If you then cross to a position on the line AB, the direction of play changes. The viewer could end up confused.

So before the match gets underway, decide which side you are going to shoot from – the line AB or the line CD. Your choice will be governed mainly by the position of the sun, which should be behind you.

If the sky is overcast, shoot towards the most attractive background. Shooting from lines AC and BD is in fact easier, because you don't have to pan so much, but you are generally further away from the action.

▶ ***A good action shot where the team in yellow is attacking the goal to the right. This is alright, so long as all the shots in the same half show the team kicking in this direction.***

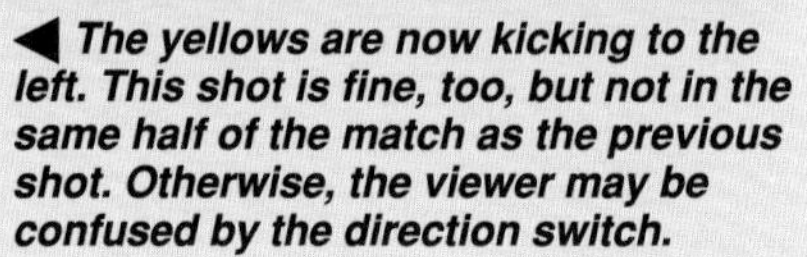

◀ ***The yellows are now kicking to the left. This shot is fine, too, but not in the same half of the match as the previous shot. Otherwise, the viewer may be confused by the direction switch.***

Edited highlights

All the shots that are both interesting and well shot should be included as 'master shots' in the final video. Don't worry if the pans are a bit jerky, so long as they follow the action.

The best way of viewing your sport video is to think of it as a selection of shots, rather than a video of the whole game. Follow the main action with the camcorder and pause whenever there is a break in play or whenever you lose track of the ball. When there is a long break, run to a different position.

Each shot you record is known as a 'master shot' because it deals with the main subject of the video – the game. When you review your tape later, make a list of all the master shots and the counter number where they appear on the tape.

Look at each shot again and tick the ones you can use. A shot can be unusable for a number of reasons. It may contain no interesting action, the autofocus system may have focused on the wrong subject, or you may have ended the shot too soon – and missed a crucial part of the action.

The master shots are the bones of your video. However, you need to add a lot more if you want a really polished result.

Cutaways

Cutaways are shots that take place near to the main action (see **The right cut**, page 77). You should shoot a lot of cutaways, as these will be useful when you come to edit.

Cutaways may be of people in the crowd, substitutes warming up on the sideline, an aeroplane flying overhead or even a player on the pitch shaking his head. Try to record shots of the crowd when it's active – shouting or cheering. Mix long shots with close-ups.

You should also shoot a few establishers – although if they come in the middle of the action they are called re-establishers. These can be long shots that show the whole ground or action on the field from a distance, or zoom out shots from a distant subject to the whole field.

Establishers and cutaways can be shot at any time. When you edit, make a list of the good cutaways and establishers too. Next, decide the shot order. The cleanest way of doing this is to make a 'rough cut' of the master shots first.

Between the last master shot and this, there is a jump, because the action has switched from one end of the pitch to the other. Split them up by using a 'cutaway'.

Start with the kick off, and copy all the good master shots in the order they were recorded. Armed with your shot list, watch your rough cut. Some cuts will look fine, but others will look poor because there is a jump in the action.

Tick the good cuts and put an 'X' by the jumps. When you produce your finished version, insert a cutaway or re-establisher wherever there is an 'X'. Now make a second shot list, starting with establishing shots of players running on to the field and warming up and moving through the master shots, cutaways and re-establishers.

Don't end the game with the final whistle – show the players walking from the field, and the reaction of the winners and losers. You could edit the shots as they now appear on your revised shot list, but there are still one or two things you can do to add professional polish to your video.

Polished finish

You can add a couple more things to make your video look professional. The first is the 'action replay'. This should be used sparingly – for instance, when you capture a goal or good save on tape.

On your shot list, repeat the counter number of those shots worthy of an action replay. Once you have copied one of these shots, recopy it – only in slow motion, if your camcorder has that facility.

The second professional touch you see on TV is titling. As it is impractical to add titles while you are shooting the match, add them during editing. Don't use too many titles though – perhaps just to introduce the teams, give updates on the scores and add action replay over the appropriate shots.

If your camcorder doesn't allow you to add titles at the editing stage and you don't have a titling unit, create title cards separately and insert them at the appropriate points.

The best way of adding this kind of title is to use a video recorder with INSERT EDIT facility. This allows you to record over part of an already recorded shot, without affecting the sound.

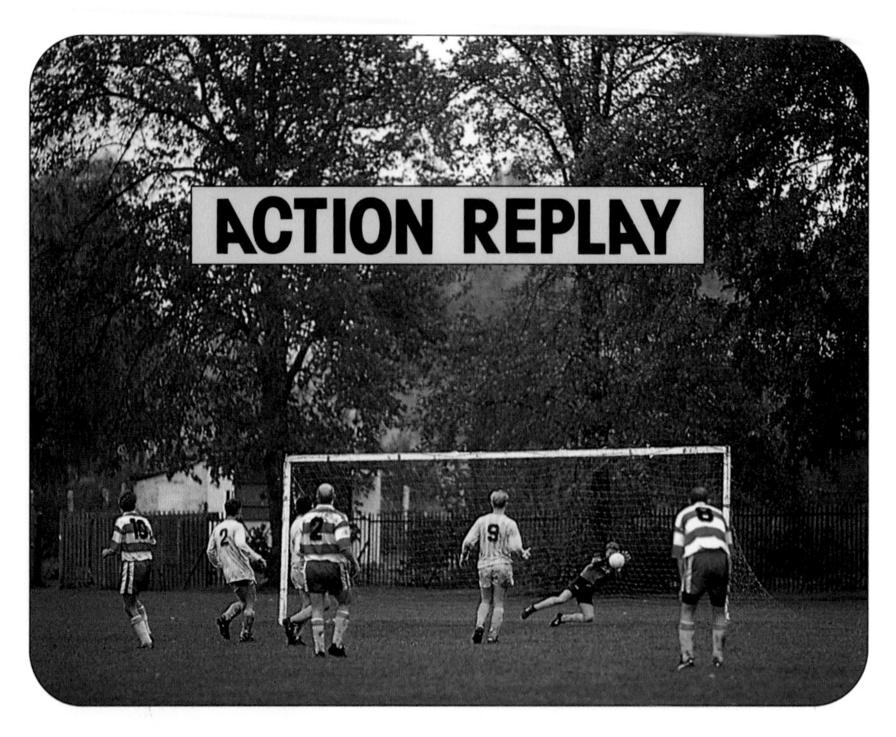

▲ ***For important shots, such as goals, copy the shot twice, but record it in slow motion the second time. Add an ACTION REPLAY title over the slow motion shot.***

Although you need the original sound – particularly the sounds of shouting and the ball being kicked – you may also want to mix in extra sound, such as a 'wildtrack' of crowd noise (see **Advanced sound techniques**, page 35) or a commentary.

Prepare a commentary beforehand, working out what you are going to say about the various shots and writing them down. If you have a hi-fi VCR, you can keep the original sound on the hi-fi tracks and dub on to the mono track.

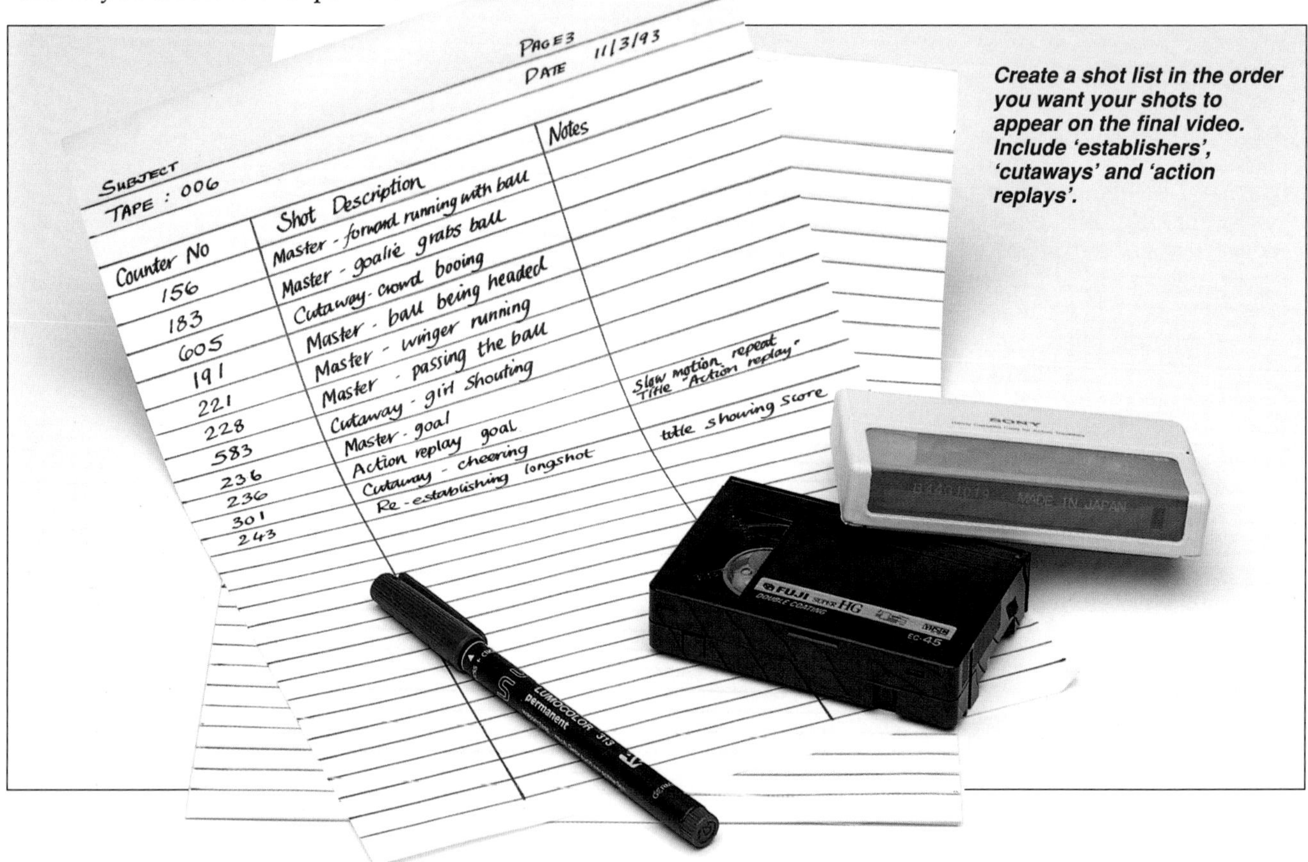

Create a shot list in the order you want your shots to appear on the final video. Include 'establishers', 'cutaways' and 'action replays'.

Applied video – Interview techniques

Interviews crop up in virtually every kind of video, from documentary to family album. Over the years, television has devised tried and tested ways of shooting them well.

▲ ***Interviews crop up in all sorts of videos. The simplest way of shooting them is to have both the interviewer and interviewee in shot. Use a microphone when recording outside.***

In some videos, interviews form the centrepiece, particularly those where you are profiling a person or those where you are presenting an argument, such as a promotional or documentary style video. But you might want to interview someone in more everyday home movies too.

If you are shooting a video of a sports match, for instance, interviewing one of the players before and after the event would make an interesting addition to the video. Similarly, it may be fun to interview a nervous starlet before a video of the school play.

The most common type of interview is the formal video, where you are trying to extract information from someone who knows about the subject. In documentary style videos, this may be an expert on the subject you are making a video about whose evidence backs up your case, but it could just as easily be a person providing general information or entertainment.

If you are questioning an expert on a subject, make sure you research the subject yourself first. Make up a list of specific questions in advance, but by knowing something about the subject, you will be able to pick up on points made by the interviewee. In any case, don't go too far off the track unless something amazing crops up.

Let the person know beforehand the kind of questions you want to ask. However, don't give them the specific questions, as this may ruin the spontaneity of the interview.

Background information

When you arrange to interview someone formally – for a documentary or campaigning video, for instance – pay a visit to the location of the interview first. This is called going on a 'recce'.

The most important thing is to check out the location yourself. Determine the best spot for the interview to take place and make sure there is enough room and the appropriate sockets for any lights you want to take along.

If possible, do a 'sound check' (see **Sound sense**, page 31), particularly if you intend to shoot the interview outdoors or in a public place. If you are shooting in a public place, make sure you obtain any appropriate permission first.

When looking for a location, choose a background that is appropriate to the subject. If you are interviewing someone about their garden, for instance, interview them by their prize exhibits. If you are campaigning against the speed of traffic on a busy road, take some shots of the road, but move away to a quieter place to conduct the interview.

When you are videoing outside, there should be fewer problems with lighting, but you may find that you need to use a reflector (see page 64). Above all, conduct the interview in a location where the interviewee feels reasonably comfortable, making sure that the background is not too cluttered.

▶ ***The location you choose for your interviews can add a lot to the video. Here, the subject is explaining about her garden, so it makes sense to film her actually in the garden. However, remember all the other rules of composition too. Leave looking room in front of her and make sure the background is uncluttered.***

Formal interviews

Check the sound and lighting for formal interviews. For sound testing, a set of headphones is essential, so that you can test what is actually being recorded.

You may be able to use the camcorder's built-in microphone, but if there is any background noise that might interfere with what the speaker is saying, use an add-on mic.

Conducting the interview is a lot easier if there are two of you to interview the subject. That way, one of you can ask the questions, while the other operates the camera. More professional set ups also have a third person to look after sound and a fourth to set up the lighting, but these aren't essential.

Use two, three or four light set ups (see page 64). A setting light is not necessary unless the person is sitting close to the background. The backlight will improve the appearance of the subject, but is not as essential as the key or fill light.

Start the interview with an establishing shot that shows both the interviewer and the interviewee. From this position you can cut back and forth, using the method described below.

Whether you position the camera slightly above, below or level with the subject's head can alter their appearance considerably (see **Camera height**, page 19). Shoot from below to increase their authority; shoot from above to make their words appear less significant.

1 ▶ ESTABLISHING SHOT
Before you move in for the main interview, shoot ten or fifteen seconds' worth of tape from behind the interviewer. By showing the interviewer and interviewee in the same shot, you establish the scene for the viewer.

The two should simply chat for the first few seconds, and the establishing shot should end with the interviewer asking the first question.

When you edit this shot, you can turn down the volume for the initial chatting and add a voice-over. Turn the volume up in time to ask the first question.

2 ◀ MAIN INTERVIEW
Explain to the interviewee about the establishing shot, so that they don't immediately start to answer the question.

The camcorder should be paused as soon as the interviewer has asked the first question. Move in as close as the interviewer and start recording again.

Ask the interviewer to repeat the question. When you edit, start this shot after the interviewer has asked the question. Zoom in and out during the interview, but make the movements discreet. The camcorder operator should know when the interesting questions are coming up, and should zoom in as soon as the interviewer asks one.

Only zoom out while the interviewer is asking a question, not while the interviewee is talking.

The set up

The person is seated at a desk, being interviewed about his company. Behind him is a wall containing appropriate material, such as a profit chart and a productivity award. Key and fill lights are positioned either side of the interviewer, well out of shot.

The camcorder positions are to the side so that the two people aren't staring straight into the lens. The camera is positioned further back for the establishing shot, which shows the interviewee over the interviewer's shoulder.

The camera moves in so it is next to the interviewer's right shoulder for the main interview and for cut-in shots of the interviewee. After the interview, the camera is moved to the left of the interviewee, so that the interviewer can repeat some of the questions and record 'noddy' shots – that is, shots of the interviewer nodding.

3 CUT-INS

Cut-ins are very similar to cutaways (see page 80), only instead of being shots of incidental subjects near the main action, they are usually close-up shots of the main subject itself.

They serve two main purposes. First, they can be inserted at points in the editing stage to hide bad zooms or jumps in the interview.

In the second place, they can tell you something about the main subject of the interview. The classic cut-in is of the interviewee's hands. If they are playing with a pencil or a necklace, for instance, it suggests that the person is nervous.

When using them in this way, insert the cut-in with the insert edit facility found on some VCRs (see page 96).

4 NODDY SHOTS

After the interview, move the camcorder to the other side of the desk and re-record the interviewer asking questions. When you edit, you can leave the interviewee on-screen while the question is asked, or cut to the interviewer.

If the question is significant, keep filming the interviewee so the viewer doesn't miss their reaction. If it's straightforward, cut back to the interviewer. Also show the interviewer to hide the fact that the camera has zoomed out or if you want to miss out a question or two.

You can also shoot 'noddy shots' from this position – shots where the interviewer nods or reacts to what is said. Like cut-ins, use them to cover potential jump cuts when you miss out some of the interviewee's answer. The interviewee can be absent when you record them.

Informal interviews

Whatever the subject of your video, you are likely at some point to shoot an informal interview. This can be anything from pointing the camcorder at a child and asking them what they want for Christmas, to roaming the streets questioning members of the public on topical issues.

Even though the interview is informal, and you may want a 'rough and ready' feel to it, it doesn't mean you can get away with an unsteady image. Use a tripod if at all possible.

Make sure your questions are easy to answer – but not too easy. The two classic mistakes are not clearly defining the topic you want the person to talk about ('say something for Auntie Jean...'), and asking a question that can be answered just by yes or no ('did you enjoy your holiday?')

Better kinds of question might be, for example: 'Tell Auntie Jean all the things you'd like for your birthday,' and 'what did you enjoy most about your holiday?'

When you are interviewing children, you may have to suggest ideas to them, but stop talking as soon as they start answering.

▲ ***Don't point the camera at a child and expect them to say something. Ask questions, but not those that can be answered with a yes or no. Handing them props, like this necklace, can also give them something to talk about.***

Vox pops

Filming members of the public to find out opinions is known as 'vox pops'. In campaigning videos or documentaries, this technique is used to reinforce the arguments you are putting forward by showing public opinion supports the stand you are taking.

Shoot the people in close-up, with just their head and shoulders showing, as anything else is a distraction. Do, however, vary the backgrounds, so that the people you have chosen to interview look like a genuine cross section.

There are two ways of approaching the presentation. The 'light' style includes the interviewer, who is armed with a microphone, which is thrust into people's faces.

The 'heavier' style comprises a series of close-ups of people, with no interviewer or mic showing in the shot. Again, don't choose questions that can be answered in one word, and don't talk when the interviewee is talking.

Wait until they have finished speaking before you ask another question – otherwise you will have difficulty editing it out.

▲ ***With vox pops, people can either talk to the camera or to an interviewer slightly off camera. When you interview more than one person, vary their position in the frame.***

Applied video – Shooting wildlife

Alfred Hitchcock advised directors never to work with animals, but this doesn't stop them making excellent video subjects.

You only have to see the popularity of wildlife programmes to realize what fascinating subjects animals can make. The most important resource when recording animals, be they your pet cat or herds of wildebeest sweeping majestically across the plain – is patience.

The next two essentials are time and planning. Videos featuring animals are often the most wasteful in terms of unused recording – you often have to shoot hours of material to get a few minutes of good footage.

Fortunately, this is not a problem with video. Tape is cheap and reusable, so unless you run out of power, you can keep recording for as long as you like. You must, of course, be prepared to edit the material later and cut out all the bad footage.

Planning is important because understanding the habits of your subject can save you time and help you identify when it is at its most appealing. If you aren't familiar with the subject, it pays to read up on it first.

Four-legged friends

Pets make the easiest subjects because their habits are familiar and they usually feel comfortable with humans. Some may even be willing subjects, particularly if some reward, such as food or affection, is on offer.

Although it is often entertaining to dress up animals, or get them to do uncharacteristic things in front of the camera, the best videos are usually those that show the animal acting most naturally.

Kittens and puppies soon get used to the camera, and you can get good shots while they are engaged in play. Dogs are often the easiest subjects, though, because they have predictable habits.

Sometimes an animal will do something hilarious that warrants grabbing the camcorder and recording immediately. But most of the time you can plan what shots you want.

A good starting point is to think of those animal characteristics or actions that you tell people about – if they make interesting anecdotes, chances are they'll make interesting footage.

As the proverb says: 'you can take a horse to water, but you can't make it drink'. You can prod or coax a cat to encourage it to move about, but you'll have a disappointing video. Cats look best when they are stalking like tigers, not when they are plodding along trying to find another quiet spot in which to curl up.

Horses are convenient to shoot because they have the same head height as humans, but with other animals, shoot from *their* head height. Shoot from below if you want to emphasize their power, but only shoot from above if you want them to look pathetic, such as a shot of a contrite puppy or an animal begging for food.

An interesting technique is to insert a couple of shots from the animal's point of view. Shoot this by holding the camcorder by your side – so that it's about level with your knees – and walk quickly.

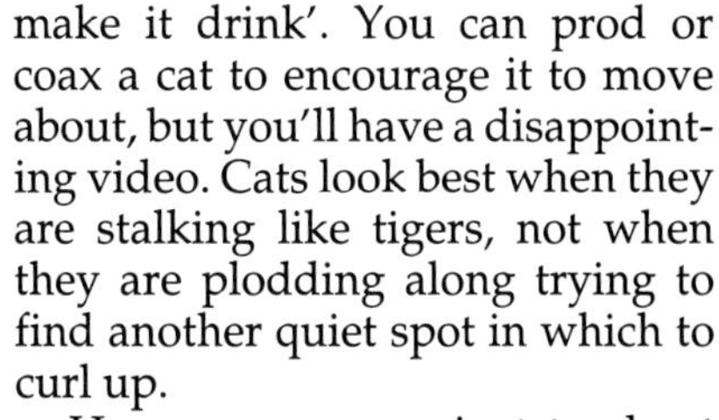

▲ ▶ ▼ ***Zooming out from the pigeon to reveal the cat is a far more interesting way of showing this scene than using a simple static shot. When you come across a good shot, think of the best way of shooting it before you start to record. As you will be using the telephoto end of the lens at the start of a zoom out, it is best to use some form of support to keep the camcorder steady. But hand hold if you would otherwise miss the shot.***

Urban wildlife

A little harder to capture on tape, but certainly no less rewarding, are semi-wild animals, such as the urban wildlife that makes its home in gardens and parks. Birds and squirrels are very common, but foxes can be found in some areas too.

The best way of attracting animals into your own garden is to use a bird table. You may need to leave food in the same place for several weeks before animals start to feed there regularly. Remember to continue feeding after the taping is complete, as animals get used to the food being available.

The key thing about a bird table is that it should be the same distance from the ground as the camcorder. The beauty of this set up is that you can use your house as a 'hide', with the camcorder mounted on a tripod and pointing out of a window at the table.

You don't even need to stand by the camcorder to watch the action. You can simply run a lead from the camcorder to your TV and watch on your television. Better still, connect it through the video recorder, and, if your camcorder allows it, record on to this, rather than on to the camcorder tape.

You can even record several hours of footage while you are out by leaving the camcorder recording. If you are shooting through glass, you will have to focus the camcorder manually, as some systems may be confused and focus on the window.

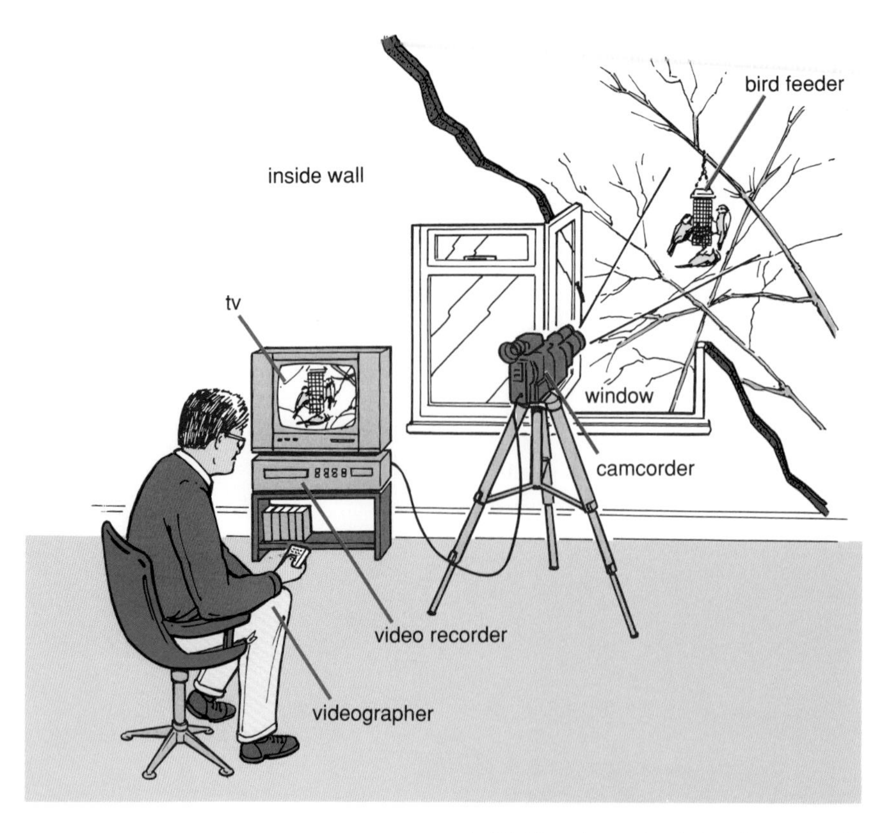

▲▼ Shooting animals is a lot easier if you know where they are going to be. That way you can set up the equipment first and sit and wait. You can ensure animals go where you want by leaving out food for them. If you are shooting in your own garden, put the camcorder inside the house, so you are shooting through a window. If it is closed, focus manually and avoid views with distracting backgrounds.

Tip: Fishy business

Fish tend to be thought of as passive subjects, but if you get close, so that they fill the screen, you can get an interesting perspective on their world.

Although ponds are more natural than fish tanks, they do have the disadvantage that you can only shoot the fish from above. Use a polarizing filter to eliminate unwanted reflections.

If you are shooting through water or glass, your AF system may be fooled. Once again, switch to manual focus.

Going to the zoo

Zoos and safari parks offer opportunities to shoot animals not otherwise accessible to most camcorder owners. However, not all animals are kept in easy to reach places, and not all are willing to perform in front of the camera.

When planning a trip to a safari park or zoo, avoid very hot days, as animals tend to sleep in such conditions. The best time to shoot is either early morning or late afternoon on a day without clouds.

Get hold of a programme, so you can plan your day. Animals get active before feeding time, and feeding itself can provide good material, as can organized displays – particularly aquatic shows. Again, use a polarizing filter.

If you are shooting tigers or lions, don't shoot from above, as the shots will have little impact. Ideally, mount the camcorder on a tripod and use the telephoto, so you can crop in tightly. Alternatively, frame a wider area and pan with them as they pace.

Zoos and safari parks are ideal locations for recording animal wildtracks on a tape recorder. These can be audio dubbed on to the edited material later.

Through the wire

Many animals at zoos, and even safari parks, are kept behind bars or wire. As with glass, wire meshing and bars can confuse the camcorder's autofocus system so that it focuses on the bars and not the animal beyond.

If you get close to the bars and focus manually on the animals, however, the bars may be thrown out of focus. This way, you get to see the animal, not the bars. To guarantee that the bars are thrown out of focus, you should try and limit the depth of field as much as possible.

You can do this by placing a neutral density (ND) filter over the lens or by setting a high shutter speed. (Both of these alternatives open the iris.) Be careful, however, not to set too high a shutter speed, or you may find you have unwanted strobing.

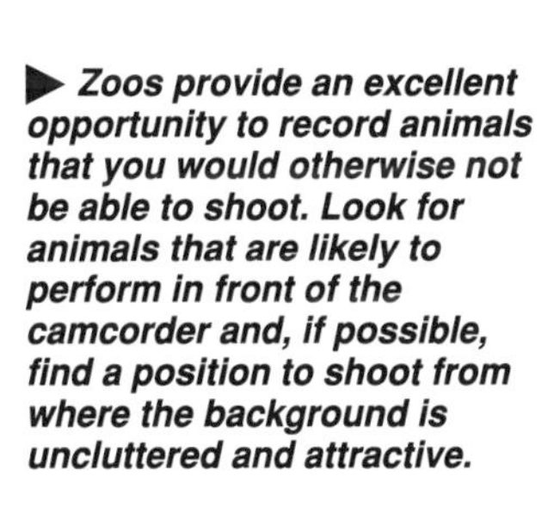

▶ Zoos provide an excellent opportunity to record animals that you would otherwise not be able to shoot. Look for animals that are likely to perform in front of the camcorder and, if possible, find a position to shoot from where the background is uncluttered and attractive.

Out and about

When you head off into the countryside to find animals in their natural habitat, make a very early start to get to likely locations before nocturnal animals retire and before the country is invaded by traffic and picnickers.

Look at guidebooks before you go, and work out the best locations. There are numerous wildlife books that give details of animal habits and locations. Binoculars make useful accessories, as they allow you to spot your subject without wasting your camcorder's battery.

In order to fill the frame with shy animals in their own habitat, use the telephoto end of your zoom or a teleconverter. Because camera shake is more evident at these high magnifications, you have to use a tripod to ensure a stable picture, so choosing your spot is important.

Official hides are positioned so they look out on to clearings that animals such as deer frequent. If you go elsewhere, make use of natural cover, setting your tripod up behind a tree or bush or even in a tent. Camouflage blankets and hats are also available.

Shoot lots of footage and edit the video later. With a wildlife video, shoot attractive locations, sunrises and pans as you see them. These help establish both the theme and the mood of the video.

Wild music

There is likely to be a very high proportion of added sound on a wildlife video, but capturing 'live' sounds is also important. Use a shotgun mic to pick up sounds from some distance away, but take a tape recorder to record a wildtrack of country sounds. This should be mixed with the live sound later.

Many wildlife videos benefit from commentary, which can be dubbed later. The two main kinds of commentary are documentary-style, where you talk about the animals, and diary-style, where you bring yourself into the programme and talk about your experiences. Remember, the most dramatic shots are when the subject fills the screen, so use the telephoto and get as close as you can.

▲ ***By finding out where animals are likely to graze, you can save yourself hours of driving around looking for locations.***

◀ ***Grey squirrels are common in parks and woodlands. They are used to people and are often friendly enough to get close to.***

◀ ***For timid creatures, such as this red deer, use a long telephoto and shoot from some natural cover, so that you can't be seen.***

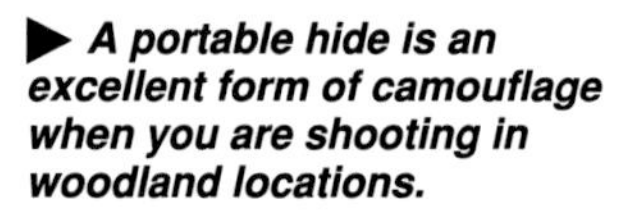

▶ ***A portable hide is an excellent form of camouflage when you are shooting in woodland locations.***

Applied video – The family album

Most stills camera users keep the best shots of their family and friends in a photo album. With video, you can create a moving family album, combining the best moments from all your videos.

As you shoot more events with your camcorder, you will eventually build up an extensive library of tapes. Even if each event is edited down to the highlights, viewing the whole collection could still take hours.

To keep all of these events fresh and convenient to view, you can create a tape of the best of your edited highlights. Add a few photographs, converted old cine film, and some new shots to link the various scenes, and you have a moving record of the important people and events in your life.

Deciding the format

Your first task is to decide the format of your family album – for instance, whether you are going to add commentary or let the images speak for themselves, and whether you are going to arrange the shots by subject or chronologically.

The second is to decide the exact shots you want to use. This is time consuming, but worth it. As you rewatch your old tapes, make a note of the bits you want, the tape they appear on and the counter number where they start.

If you have a children's party video that lasts for 20 minutes, only use a few of the shots. Similarly, from a wedding, choose only the crucial images – some from the ceremony itself and maybe a few key sentences from the speeches.

If you want a 'scrapbook' album, mix the interesting images as you please. If you want to set about a more ambitious project, tackle the events chronologically, breaking up each one by using title cards naming either the year or the event.

▶ ***You may have a collection of videos that cover subjects as diverse as holidays, family events and school plays. The highlights can be combined on a video family album.***

On the rostrum

If you are creating a video family album, you may want to include events that took place before camcorders became widely available. You can do this by incorporating other memorabilia into your video, such as prints from a stills camera or newspaper cuttings.

To keep the camcorder and the object you are videoing level, use a table as a makeshift rostrum. Make sure the object you are copying is firmly fixed in position and flat on to the camcorder.

The camcorder should be placed on a tripod or a pile of books. You may be able to light the object with window light, but make sure you don't get any shadow from the camcorder. Ideally, the object should be lit from both sides of the camcorder. Low powered video lights can be used, but directional desk lamps are fine.

If you are shooting a mounted print, such as an old school photograph, remove the glass from in front of it before you start recording. Otherwise, the light will cause hot spots – intense areas of reflection on the photograph. If the print is glossy, so that it causes reflections even when the glass is removed, try re-positioning the lights to eliminate the reflections.

Zoom out

Rather than show a large photograph in one go, try cutting between close-up details of individual pupils. Alternatively, zoom in from a wide shot to the important person in the shot, or track along a row of pupils.

It may be easier to move the print than the camcorder. Do this by mounting it on a board and sliding it past the lens. To magnify the image enough so that a small portion of the print fills the frame, you may have to use the camcorder in macro mode.

If you have a tripod that allows you to shoot directly down on a subject, you may be able to show newspaper clippings in a creative way. Place the page on a piece of cardboard on a record turntable and position the camcorder above.

Start the turntable rotating and slowly zoom in, so the newspaper appears to move towards the camcorder. This technique works best if there is a prominent headline or photograph that can even be seen when the paper is rotating.

▶ When videoing flat subjects, such as this old school photo, make sure the subject and the camcorder are held steady. Use two lamps for even lighting.

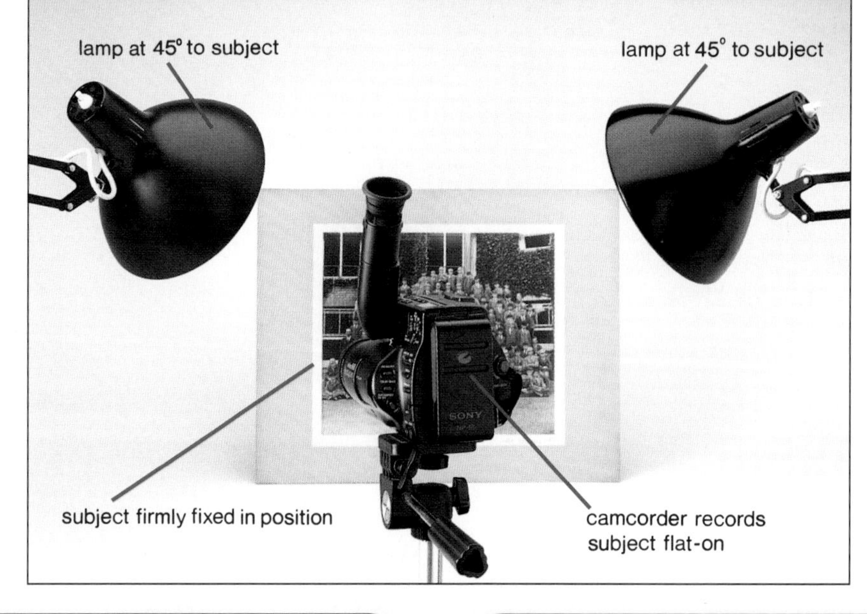

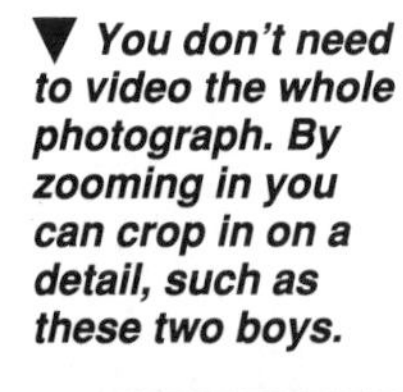

▼ You don't need to video the whole photograph. By zooming in you can crop in on a detail, such as these two boys.

▼ By sliding the subject slowly past the lens, you can examine each person in the photograph in detail.

Film to video

You may also have old slides and cine that you want to include in your video. The simplest method is to project the slide or cine footage on to a screen and video directly off this. Turn off all other lights in the room and set the camcorder's white balance system to the indoor 'tungsten' setting.

It is important to project a small, bright image, say about 12cm wide, to enable the camcorder to record at a reasonably high light level.

Distortion

Take care to position the camcorder absolutely square-on to the screen, or else the image might be distorted slightly. Such distortion is known as 'keystoning'. Connect the camcorder to the TV during recording to monitor the quality.

If you are recording sound from cine, connect the audio output from the projector to the audio input of the camcorder (if it has one). If not, link the camcorder to the VCR and record directly on to the VCR.

The projector's audio output then plugs into the VCR's audio in. Don't plug the audio out into the camcorder's microphone input except through a special attenuator lead.

▶ ***Simple telecine units can take the hard work out of film-to-video transfer. Cine or slides are projected in through one aperture and the camcorder records through another.***

Film attachments

There are more advanced methods of transferring cine and slides to video without using a projection screen. The simplest is to place a slide close to the lens with a light source behind it and set the camcorder to macro mode.

Ensure the camcorder and slide are fixed in one position and either mask off the space between the slide and the end of the lens with card or black tape, or else turn off all other light sources in the room so they don't affect exposure.

An alternative is to use a dedicated slide adaptor which you can attach to the end of the lens in the same way as you attach a teleconverter.

The best method of transferring slide or cine to video is with a telecine transfer unit. With this the films are projected through a screen in the side of a box. On another side of the box is a small window through which the image is projected. When the camcorder is placed in front of this window, it can record the image directly.

Telecine transfer boxes can be used to transfer prints, slides or cine to video.

Cropping slides

TV uses a 4:3 format, whereas 35mm slides use a 3:2 aspect ratio, so you can't frame each slide exactly. Frame the most interesting part of the slide.

If it is a vertical 'portrait' format slide, either crop even tighter or tilt the camcorder up or down the image. There will be a reduction in quality when you shoot from a projection screen, so remember, the closer you crop in on a photo, the greater the degree of magnification and the lower the quality of the image.

Technological approach

▲ ***The Tamron Fotovix can convert slides or negatives to video. A basic processor allows colour correction. Results can be viewed on TV.***

More advanced units that can be used for slide transfer include the Fotovix and Photo CD. The first is shaped like a microscope. Slides or negatives are placed in a tray beneath the lens, and Fotovix converts these to video images. A processor is built into the unit.

Photo CD players are similar to compact disc players, but they can also read photographic images from a gold Photo CD. These images can be placed directly on to disc by a processing lab when you have your film developed. It is also possible to have existing pictures transferred on to disc by a lab.

Photo CD players have a variety of video outputs, so they can be connected directly to a video recorder. Compact Disc-Interactive (CD-I) players can also play back Photo CDs.

▲ ***Kodak's Photo CD players can play back gold CDs containing photographic images. Pictures have to be transferred to CD by a film processor.***

Back in time

A more ambitious project than highlights of your collected videos and still photographs is to create a family history video. This might mean starting the story several decades ago and shooting new footage of relevant subjects – such as houses where your parents or grandparents were born.

A good starting point is to have the most senior member of your family talking into the camcorder. Their commentary can provide the audio track over photographs or location shots. If houses where they used to live no longer exist, ask them to explain what their home used to be like.

Interview several people who are important in your life – or the life of your family. Ask them if they have any old photos or cine footage. If you don't want to transfer the cine by either of the methods suggested, or you don't have the equipment, there are specialists who will transfer the film to video for you.

As you bring your story more up to date, you will be able to use more of your camcorder footage. To link the scenes, add a commentary, which should be prepared and recorded on to audio tape before you start. As a family album is personal, it may be best for you to read the linking passages yourself.

Whenever possible, let the people you interview tell the story for themselves. Show somebody talking about a person or event, then insert a photo of the event. You don't have to find an end to the video, as it can be added to as time goes on.

▲ ***A good way of introducing old footage is to start with a new recording of someone talking to camera about the event.***

Insert edit

Some video recorders allow you to 'insert edit' a new piece of video over a previously recorded shot, while retaining the mono sound track of the original. The benefit of this facility is that you can record one long shot – say of a person sitting in a chair reminiscing – that lasts for a minute or more.

By using the insert edit facility, you can insert brief images over the long shot to illustrate what the person is saying. This is visually far more interesting than seeing the narrator for all that time, while the monologue provides continuity to the sequence. On some video recorders, this facility is called 'video insert' or 'video dub'.

▶ ***Insert the old footage next. If you use the 'insert edit' facility, you can continue with the commentary while the cine is on screen.***